PROTECTING CHILDREN IN EUROPE: TOWARDS A NEW MILLENNIUM

EDITED BY:
MARGIT HARDER & KEITH PRINGLE

AALBORG UNIVERSITY PRESS

PROTECTING CHILDREN IN EUROPE

© 1997 Aalborg University Press and the Authors

Cover design by Roland Jensen

Printed in Denmark by Schølin Grafisk

ISBN 87-7307-549-3

Aalborg University Press
Badehusvej 16
DK-9000 Aalborg
Denmark

Tlf: +4598 130915
Fax: +4598 134915

Contents

Introduction

By Margit Harder and Keith Pringle

Protecting Children in Europe: Towards a New Millennium, is a publication concerning child protection in five European countries: Denmark, England and Wales, Finland, Ireland and Italy.

The title expresses the book's three-fold purpose:
Description and analysis of *child protection* in the five countries in its historical context as well as in modern times. A certain weight is attached to child abuse which includes physical and psychological abuse and neglect as well as sexual abuse.
Each chapter also contains the authors' conceptions of future developments (*Towards a New Millennium*). Even if the Danish humorous writer Robert Storm Petersen said: "Predictions are difficult, especially as they concern the future", a view into the future, based on analysis of developments up to the present, has been carried out. Thoughts about the future expressed here are not necessarily a reflection of each specific country's officially stated intentions.
Europe in this book does not mean Europe literally, i.e. all countries of Northern, Eastern, Central and Western Europe are not represented. It does not even mean the European Union. Titles of books, however, cannot be limitless. Therefore, "Europe" in this connection just means the five mentioned countries.

All five countries are members of the European Union. In fact, their common membership is one main reason for this publication as it is one of the results of an Erasmus project.

The Erasmus programme was (similar programmes are now called Socrates) an inter-university co-operation under the European Union concerning student and teaching staff mobility and curriculum development. All the contributors have been participating in the programme. As one theme of the curriculum development was child care, the co-operation resulted, amongst other things, in this publication. We found our cooperation extremely interesting and found it inspiring to get some insight in social policy and child protection from other countries. Actually, our perspectives on our own society were given extra and more subtle dimensions.

Another main reason for this book is the authors' engagement in children and their conditions of life. We have all practised and/or studied child care and child protection. Our countries have ratified the United Nations' Convention of Childrens' Rights and thus these states have undertaken special obligations to children.

Even if the background for the represented countries is an existing Erasmus/-Socrates programme, it so happened that the contributing countries do represent contrasting "types" of welfare systems.

It could entail a long discussion to define types of systems in Europe. Many models have been developed to describe differences, especially between the systems within the European Union.

A two-model explanation of the differentiations between EU-states can be seen in the 1991 work of the EU Commission (Abrahamson 1993). This makes a distinction between the Beveridge and the Bismarck models, the former named after the person who created Britain's social policy reform in the 1940's; whilst Bismarck created, at the end of 19th century, a labour market based social insurance system. This is a simple distinction.

A three-model explanation has been drawn up by Esping-Andersen (1990a) who suggested a distinction between conservative, liberal and social-democratic states. This, and also the Habermas (1985) three-model distinction (in liberal/conservative, corporative/social-democratic and zero-growth/red-green models) have been criticised as too limited. Bislev/Hansen (1990) and Leibfried (1992) suggest supplementing them with a fourth model: the Latin or Catholic one. A communist and a post-communistic Eastern European model (Abrahamson 1993) could be added to provide an explanation of six models.

All are ideal type models and as such present problems regarding "reality". Speaking about social policy they can all be criticised as for example by Pringle (forthcoming) on the grounds that they ignore dimensions of disadvantage such as gender; race/culture; disability; sexuality; age etc.

However, there are obvious differences between the countries presented in this book.

Denmark and Finland are known as belonging to the Scandinavian welfare model. Briefly explained, this means that social welfare is based on universal service, in principle obtainable by any citizen. Social welfare is first and foremost financed by public taxes and instituted by public staff. Welfare policy is an element in providing equal rights and possibilities to every citizen. Thus, for instance education for children and youngsters as well as the health system are independent of personal income.

Britain is as the Nordic countries characterized by universal tax-financed social welfare. The benefits are low compared to the Nordic benefits, i.e. they contain an element of stigmatization for the users. The system is furthermore based on supplementary private insurances. Voluntary and private social work is growing. Ireland and Italy are, in relation to social policy, organized in a social support hierarchy (Abrahamson 1993). The individual is expected to take care of him(her)self and his(her) family. If more assistance is necessary the family network is expected to intervene. And then other relations and/or local social networks, for instance the Catholic Church may be called upon. It is also expected that the citizens are insured against social events. The public social welfare system is the last authority to be used when every other possibility has been exhausted. The public system is thus a final supplement to the private network. This model results in dependency on regional and local organizations more than on national forms of assistance.

These descriptions should not be seen as static. Social policy in these countries is moving as a result of cooperation in the European Union. The Scandinavian model now tends to use more voluntary and private social work and to underline the labour market's responsability for the welfare of citizens. At the same time the Mediterranian countries are now more interested in a universal and public tax-financed system as represented in, for instance, Britain and the Nordic countries. The exchange of social solutions between countries has been called the welfare-mix.

It is not easy to mix one country's solutions regarding social problems with other countries'. Even within Western Europe there are conspicuous differences between the countries as to history, tradition, politics, ideology and religion. Social issues are closely connected with the country in which they are created and defined as social problems. Even if a country might be inspired to read or hear about how other countries are taking up challenges in the social area, interventions or solutions have to respect and fit in with the culture they are transferred to.

While writing this book the question of protecting children has become an issue of central and cross-national concern since several, and obviously developing, cases of sexual abuse to children have been disclosed recently. These scandals have underlined the ongoing discussion about how to protect children against abuse within, as well as outside, their families.

Our target audience are mainly students, teaching staff and professionals in "social work" (as widely understood). We hope that other groups with responsibility for children and their families will also be inspired by this book.

Construction of the book: After this introduction follow, in alphabetical order, chapters concerning child protection in Denmark, England and Wales, Finland, Ireland and Italy. National comparisons regarding critical issues are made in the concluding chapter, where discussion about future welfare trajectories is also provided. Contributors are responsible only for the views expressed in their own pieces.

A last remark: The authors have not been obliged to write this book, nor have they been paid. The work has been done to share our thoughts and ideas in a, for us, important area. We hope you will find this book as interesting to read as we have found it to write.

References

Abrahamson, P.: "Socialpolitikmodeller i Europa: forskelle og konvergens" i Nordisk Sosialt Arbeid nr. 1, 1993.

Bislev, S./Hansen, H.: "The Nordic Welfare State and the Single European Market", in "The Nordic Countries in the Internal Market of the EEC", ed. by Lyck, L., Copenhagen, Handelshøjskolens forlag, 1990.

Esping-Andersen, G.: "Three Worlds of Welfare Capitalism", Cambridge, Polity Press, 1990a.

Habermas, J.: "Den nya oöverskådligheten - Välfärdsstatens kris och utopi", Ord och Bild 1985.

Leibfried, S.: "Towards a European Welfare State" in "Social Policy in a Changing Europe", ed. by Ferge, Z./Kolberg, J.E., Wien: Campus, 1992 .

Pringle, K.: "Children and Social Welfare in Europe", Open University Press (forthcoming).

Child Protection in Denmark

By Margit Harder

Introduction

This chapter concerns child protection in Denmark. Thus, children in distress is the main focus. Children can be distressed for many reasons. Of special interest here is society's intervention (and the background for it) in childrens' lives when their families are judged to be inadequate parents. It appears that, throughout the ages, the perception of threat against children has moved from primarily a problem associated with poverty to a question of specific families' incapability to care for their own children.

The chapter is divided in five parts. The first part tells the early history of distressed children. The second part describes and analyses the development from the 1960's until present time. This is the period of recognition of child abuse and neglect. The third part presents the current status including statistics and essential laws. The results of intervention (positive and negative) in families are dealt with in the fourth part. In the fifth part perspectives for the future will be discussed.

History of distressed children

Even if this section starts about 1600 (by the "invention" of childhood) it has to be noticed that the first written law of Denmark (Jyske Lov 1241 - covering only some parts of Denmark) included child protection in the family, as it prohibited the use of weapons in child rearing. Children were mentioned in the same breath as wives and servants. The background for the prohibition must have been too many children, wounded or killed by their families. At approximately the same time some articles were promulgated (Nielsen, 1991) by the archbishop Anders Sunesen about severe sexual abuse (mentioned for the first time in Danish sources) between father and daughter, mother and daughter, son and mother (and also persons who had intercourse with two sisters): "to consider the circumstances and then either send the involved persons to the apostolic seat or impose a penance of fourteen years". Physical abuse of children by their families thus belonged to the temporal law and sexual abuse to the church.

The 17th and 18th centuries were characterized by economic crises, and therefore difficulty, especially for the (great) poverty-stricken part of the population. Many families were not able to take care of their children and it is estimated that, at the beginning of the period, 10% of all children were begging and stealing, often together with poor and invalid adults (Sigsgaard, 1982).

Society's reaction was to remove the children to special institutions where they, as the first group in Denmark, were under edict (1619) to wear special suits so that they could be recognised as runaways (Løkke, 1989). This attempt to "save" the children from insufficient parents was not especially succesful as the mortality rate in the institutions was extremely high.

As to abuse of children, the first law covering all Denmark (Christian V's Danske Lov 1683) repeated the previous prohibition against use of weapons in child rearing. Corporal punishment was however accepted to a high degree as the same law described how children's unwanted behaviour had to be punished.

On the other hand the same law contained an unambiguous prohibition of sexual assaults on children (consanguineous - sexual relations between father/son were also mentioned here). The system of penalties included death (for both involved) by beheading and burning. (In the centuries to come the punishment was softened so that the punishment in the first Penal Act (1866) changed the frame of penalty for sexual assaults to penitentiary (the violator) and corporal punishment (the child). In the Penal Act of 1930 the child below 18 years could not longer be punished. In 1967 this age limit disappeared).

Poverty was still a condition of life for a great part of the population. During the 18th century lots of families from the country moved to the towns in the hope of better lives. The result was often even worse. Copenhagen organized in 1799 the Fattigplan (Plan of Poverty) to counteract the growing poverty. The city was divided in districts, each with a director of support (unpayed) to take care of the poorest individuals and families. The support was given partly for humanistic, partly for economic reasons. The plan of poverty was expanded to cover all Denmark in 1803.

At the end of the 19th century (the time of industrialization in Denmark) the children of the proletariat were considered as a valuable economic factor for families because of the contribution to the family's survival, and for factories as more than half of the workers were children (Sigsgaard 1982). But, gradually, the children tended to oust the adult workers and the consequences for the children's health because of the hard work began to be a problem, not only for themselves but also for the factories as the surviving children appeared to be worn out even before adulthood. A growing consciousness of rights among the workers meant that they started to express their worry for the children's health. And, at the same time industrialization had resulted in the availability of cheaper machines.

Child protection seriously started in 1873 with a prohibition against using children below 10 years in industry and some rules concerning working hours for the older ones. This took place at the same time as "the first social reform" in Denmark. The laws regarding poverty and old age pensions were necessary assistance to the most deprived but also an insurance against social disturbances. The first social reform was inspired by, in particular, The Charity Organization Society, established in England and USA at the end of the 18th century (Davis, 1964) partly arising out of German experiences concerning poor citizens.

So, until the end of the 19th century, the role of the state as to childhood changed from a defensive one: first removal of the poor and miserable, later a modest economic and slightly personal support - to an offensive role: to protect children's capacity for work.

But these steps did not solve the problem of poverty and the proletariat's children had to commit crimes to compensate for the restricted possibilities of work. Many children were in prison. At the end of the century (1893) a commission was appointed to examine the causes of children's crimes in order to prevent them (Goll, 1940). The basis for the work was that children belonged to their parents unless special circumstances made their remaining at home impossible (Horsten, 1970). This was strongly inspired by Norway's Children Act in 1896, followed by Sweden in 1902. And so was the special Scandinavian construction of a committee (to make decisions regarding children's placements outside their homes) consisting of a majority of elected members (Ydebo, 1988). The commission's work resulted in The Children's Act 1905 (Børneloven). The intention of the law was to offer a better upbringing for "criminal and neglected children", i.e. the idea of prevention was now introduced. Both criminal and supposed criminal children were the focus. And so were children who played truant or were lazy at school. One possibility was compulsory removal from the home. Institutions to fulfil the purpose were established. The degree of corporal punishment in the institutions was regulated. The children were often mistreated in the institutions. In 1912, Peter Sabroe, social democrat and member of the Folketing (Parliament) (Horsten, 1970) brought a miserable institutionalized child to the Folketing to convince the members about the intolerable conditions. The mortality rate thereafter fell.

So, child policy changes from punishment and imprisonment to (compulsory) treatment.

In the following decades Denmark was characterised by severe cut backs in social services - because of the economic world crisis and the derived mass unemployment and increased need of social security. And, partly to prevent social disturbances, the second social reform of 1933 was instituted.

A few years later formal education of social workers started (1937). Social work had of course been carried out long before that, especially by women from the upper classes. It was realized that economic support was important but not sufficient. Counselling and guidance were also essential. The hospitals (doctors) were the first to realize this and offered to the patients social assistance from unpaid staff (women). The profession of social work is thus characterized by close relations with existing social problems and also with the development of the welfare state since the end of the 1930's. Of special importance for the content of education was Mødrehjælpen (Assistance to Mothers), established because of the falling number of children. The law concerning Mødrehjælpen demanded staff with knowledge of human beings to judge resources and possibilities and with the ability to give social and medical counselling together with an intimate knowledge of social and family laws. This was the basis of social work as we also know it today: material support combined with social counselling and treatment. The latter was inspired by American social casework (Goll, 1990).

Back to the social reform: this also included the state taking responsibility for (some) children by supervising special groups, for instance children born outside marriage, children of parents receiving public economic support, adopted children. In 1961 these sections were transferred unchanged to a new law concerning children's welfare (Lov om børne- og ungdomsforsorg) (Løkke, 1989). This provoked reactions especially from psychologists and pedagogical staff who, amongst other professional groups, had for a considerable time questioned the pinpointing of low-income families as being especially risky for their children. Social engagement with the families' conditions was also supported by the growing prosperity of society. The labour market was in need of more working power and consequently the social laws softened. The 1961-law was revised in 1964 and the sections in dispute disappeared. The law emphasized the obligation to offer guidance and counselling (on a voluntary basis) to families in need of special support. According to a departemental circular (11.10.1968) such families could be: single parents, families with serious diseases: physical, psychological or mental, with parents in prison, unemployed parents, parents with alchohol problems, families on transfer income etc., i.e. a list very similar to the risk groups mentioned in the previous law but with the important difference that not every family with these characteristics was supposed to be in need of guidance and that acceptance of assistance was voluntary. But the law also contained the obligation on all citizens to inform the local social authority of children at risk.

The central position of the local social authories in child protection was followed by increasing employment of social workers. The picture of the social worker as a person employed in the Mødrehjælpen, in hospitals, in institutions for mentally disabled persons, in prisons etc. changed to social workers employed by the social services in the municipalities. This change resulted in the tradition of casework being linked with the tradition of administration (Lingås, 1993).

> This is the change in child policy from control of children and parents to counselling and support of the family when needed. And it is also the change from focus on the child's behaviour to the conditions of the whole family.

This intention was transferred to the actual Social Act (Bistandsloven) of 1976 which emphasizes the necessity for respectful intervention in families.

Development from the end of the 1960's till the 1990's

In many ways the 1960's was an extremely interesting period for Danish society. The society was economically rich, most of the citizens shared the prosperity. The main conception was that prosperity was a permanent fact. This conception resulted in consideration of central values. The end of the decade was the time of "revolution". The students revolted against the professors, the insane against the treatment in the hospitals, the adolescents against marriage and the traditional family structure etc. It is interesting that the revolutionary period reached the majority of social workers considerably later: in the middle of the 1970's. But amongst some psychologists and social workers radical theories were developed and to a certain degree also radical practice. This took place along with development of different types of family therapy. The latter development must presumably be seen as a result of an economically prosperous society with actually very few restraints in material support for the relatively few families in need. The radical period in social work appeared unfortunately to be a short and soon forgotten parenthesis presumably because of the following economic stagnation.

As to child abuse and neglect the 1960's are characterized by sparse interest and few reports on child abuse and neglect were published. Henry Kempe's work (Kempe/Helfer, 1968) clearly inspired these reports. They all draw upon limited material and they are almost all written by medical doctors. The reports deal first and foremost with physical abuse and, to a very small extent, sexual abuse. It is characteristic for this decade's reports that the children are mostly below three years, that they are all severely damaged, that they belong to socially underprivileged families and that the violators are considered as aggressive, abnormal persons (Goll/Harder, 1986). This is often seen in the first process of a society's acknowledgement of child abuse and neglect. The reports did not have public impact and also very limited impact among professional staff.

But in the **1970**'s the process of acknowledgement went further.
The first public acknowledgement of the fact that children can be mistreated in their homes is a little leaflet from Socialstyrelsen (The Social board) in 1973 which emphasizes the obligation in the 1961-law on any citizen to inform the local social authority of children at risk.
A cross-professional meeting, called "The tribunal" regarding violence against children took place in 1973. It debated the traditional parental right to inflict corporal punishment. This parental right was not directly expressed in any law but influenced both child rearing and also the Courts' convictions in cases of child abuse. The tribunal resulted in a resolution that the Government should forbid this right and also initiate a campaign concerning the damaging consequences of violence towards children. The meeting was initiated by a journalist, Frode Muldkjær[1] which undoubtedly contributed to the coming public and professional awareness of the problem. (The discussions on parental rights went on for years

and resulted in 1986 in an addition to the Custody Law, stating that parents are obliged to protect their children against physical and psychological violence as well as against any other encroachment. The section is not criminalized).

Thereafter, books (especially about corporal abuse) appeared. Most of them describe the problems, a few try to explain them. Outstanding is Kopart/Sørensen (1977) which, based particularly on German, but also American literature, refers to child abuse as a problem of integration, i.e. children's position in a violence-producing society with tendencies to discharge aggression in the nuclear family. Dealing with a severe problem, visible on an individual level, at a societal level is of course difficult in terms of action. Thus, the book influenced the understanding of child abuse and neglect, but intervention still took place at a family and child level.

Another important signal of growing awareness was the establishment of prevention groups in almost all counties of Denmark. The first group was established 1978 in Northern Jutland, inspired especially by Norwegian and Swedish experiences[2] and produced a pattern for similar groups. The prevention groups still exist and have been of great importance as regards general and specific information on the subject and specialized counselling of professional staff.

The 1970's was also the decade of the third social reform which is still the basis for the present social security rules. The purpose of the law was to offer assistance on a basis of an understanding of the social problem and its causes. It was launched under these headings: prevention, rehabilitation, growth and security. It was prepared in a period of prosperity but realized (after the first oil crisis 1971) in a period of "depression". The (social worker's) estimate of what every citizen in social trouble needed from the social security system was essential. Because of economic stagnation social problems increased. And so did the expenses for the social security system. This resulted in limits for the professional estimate. A ceiling was soon put over the free estimate, i.e. social needs were generalized instead of individualized.

And, as earlier mentioned, social workers reconsidered social work's position in society. Issues such as: Is it possible to be employed by the public system and at the same time be the client's advocate? Can social problems be solved by individualization? Which factors in society and the labour market create social problems? were questioned. In social education the society was in focus and not the individual or the family.

In the 1970's Denmark became a member of the European Common Market which certainly influenced social policy.

From the early **1980**'s (called the poor 80's) the engagement and interest in child abuse was obvious but only in professional circles. Rather many (but limited) research studies were carried out, still first and foremost by medical doctors and concerning physical abuse.

In 1981 the recommendations of the Børnekommissionen (the Childrens' Commission, appointed by the Government) were published. The Børnekommis-sionen presented valuable and extensive contributions for improving childrens' conditions of life (1981). Of special interest here is that the Commission found corporal punishment in child rearing non-acceptable but at the same time found criminalization of the relationship between parents and children inappropriate.

It was now that the awareness of sexual abuse began. Danish (female) psycholo-gists and therapists brought American experiences to Denmark. A seminar (followed by a publication (Backe et al, 1983)) took place in 1982. As a participa-tor myself (among mostly women) I see the seminar as an extremely vulnerable and emotional experience in terms of realizing that sexual abuse actually could and did happen, including in Denmark. This seminar opened the eyes of persons who had used emotional resources to cope with the fact that children could be physically damaged in their homes and now had to go through those emotions once more to also accept the fact of sexual abuse. Undoubtedly, this process was even harder because of the taboo (religious, juridical conception of the family) attached to it.
The fact that recognition of sexual abuse sapped energy from the professionals dealing with family issues can also be seen from the fact that physical violence against children tended to attract considerably less interest thereafter.

1983 also proved to be a break-through in the recognition of child abuse and neglect. The first Nordic seminar on Child Abuse and Neglect took place initiated by the pediatrician Joav Merrick.[3] It was followed by a publication (Merrick, 1985). Nordic professional engagement turned out to be overwhelming. The need to learn from other Nordic experiences was obvious. The seminars were and are cross-professional and cross-sectoral and have been of great importance in developing methods in the area.

Research on childhood became of special interest. The Socialstyrelsen (Social Board) initiated a nationwide survey (Bøgh/Parkvig, 1989) on all research projects, followed by conferences and seminars.

This took place at the same time as social work generally was influenced by economic stagnation. Increasing groups of citizens were unemployed and in need of social assistance. There was a debate (still ongoing) concerning the extent of the welfare state and public attention to groups receiving transfer income. Social workers and other professional groups were exposed to severe criticism. The state reacted by initiating social experiments (followed by a series of reports). The SUM-programme started. For social workers this development resulted in roughly two types of employment: one group of social workers were working in experimental projects and were expected to be creative and non-bureaucratic while another group remained in the administrative offices with a massive increase in new clients. The last group was also the group with the central responsibility for offering assistance to families in trouble.

Of special importance in the child area was a committee, set up by Folketing (Parliament) to reconsider the Bistandslovens (Social Act's) rules concerning children. The committee was asked to improve law and order especially in connection with placement of children. The committee based its work (1990) on experiences from families as well as professionals. The report resulted in revision of the rules. The distinction between voluntary and compulsory placement of children was clarified. Law and order regarding children as well as parents was improved.

So the 1980's are characterized by increasing social problems in general and severe efforts to solve those problems. As to child abuse and neglect consciousness became focused first and foremost on sexual abuse with a tendency to forget physical abuse.

The social focus of the **1990**'s is on marginalized groups. The development of extraordinary budgets for special groups goes on. The Folketinget (Parliament) spends great amounts in creating new ways of handling social problems with old people, people with mental health difficulties, children living on the streets, families in social need etc. And Denmark ratified the Convention of Children's Rights (1991).

At the same time two cases concerning child abuse and neglect came to massive public attention.

The "Roum-case" (Roum is the name of the village where the events took place) concerned sexual abuse against two children (siblings), a girl and a boy with severe learning disabilities. The children disclosed (when treated by a therapist) sexual abuse by family and neighbours. Six persons were convicted, amongst them the mother, in 1990. In 1991 a lawyer in cooperation with wellknown doctors requested Den Særlige Klageret (a Danish court of appeal) to take up again the conviction because of procedural error. In 1995 a new jury actually repeated the earlier conviction but the juridical judges disregarded the jury's decision. Only one person (who had confessed) was convicted.

The "Rødovre-case" (also a place name) concerned neglect. A leader of a social security office in the Copenhagen-area was in 1993 charged for not having fulfilled her obligations on behalf of the municipality to supervise four children (siblings) in their home. One of the children were found, soiled in his own faeces, in his very dirty home, by the police. The leader was aquitted later in 1993 as the Court was not sure of the duration of the situation and also because of the social services' previous economic and supportive intervention in the family. Furthermore, the leader had informed the Social Welfare Committee (politicians) of the troubles in the family. Late in 1993 the case was put on appeal to a higher court which maintained the aquittal (even if the agreement between the judges was not complete).

These cases were of great importance to developments in the child abuse and neglect area. The "Roum-case" could easily be seen as a backlash reaction against a threatening uncovering of sexual abuse over a very limited span of years. The case included aspects which many people found difficult to believe or did not want to believe. The "Rødovre-case" emphasized the dilemmas between voluntary and compulsory social assistance to families and also the schism between the social needs of children and parents. It also underlined the problems of interpreting the law. An uncertainty amongst the professional staff about how to handle child abuse and neglect was inevitable.

Actual status:

Statistics about children generally

A govermental committe concerning children (Chairman: the social minister) initiated the first collection of statistics of children as individuals (not only as family members) (Kampmann/Nielsen, 1995).

Almost half of children are born outside marriage. But almost 9 out of 10 1-year old children live with both their parents, i.e. marriage is not considered as a necessity in Denmark. 83% of all children live in families with two parents. 1/3 of the children will, in the course of their childhood, experience divorce between parents. 16% are children of single parents (90% mothers). About 1/4 of the single mothers are unemployed or pensioned. For single fathers the figure is 10%. Almost half of the families have 1 child, 2/5 have 2 and only 10% have 3 or more children.

Statistics about children in need of special support

Approximately 24.500 families received in 1993 special support to children and youngsters. 1/5 of the support was given to avoid the childrens' placement outside home. By the end of 1994 (latest figures) 11.850 children were placed outside home. It is estimated that 5-6.000 of the children are placed due to severe troubles in their homes (Andersen, 1989, Larsen/Ydebo, 1994). Numerically this is a fall but a new method of registrering the figures (from 1.1.1993) and a falling number of children in the general population actually means that, relatively, the figures for children below 12 years have not changed during the last decade (1411 children between 0-6 years are placed outside home, and so are 2167 children between 7-11 years). The share of children placed without the wish and will of their parents (and possibly themselves) has increased from 3,2% of all placements in 1985 to 7,9% in 1994. Most of the children (especially below 12 years) are placed in foster families, and the second largest group in 24-hours institutions. The increase in compulsory placements was expected because of more specific instructions in the Bistandsloven, even if the increase seems larger that it actually is because of the earlier mentioned change in registration.

Immigrants' children are, as shown in a Copenhagen research concerning compulsory placements (Ertmann, 1994), at the same level as other children placed without their parents' wish and will. However, there are some dissimilarities as the immigrants' children are older than other placed children at the first placement and they move back sooner into their families. It is likely that the situation will change in the future as figures from neighbour-countries (Sweden and Norway) show that immigrants' children are overrepresented in statistics of placement (Skytte, 1997).

Actual important laws concerning families and children

The duties and the rights of parents towards their children are established in **Myndighedsloven** (law concerning custody). Of special interest is § 2,2 which obliges the parents to protect their children against physical and psychological violence as well as other encroachments. As earlier mentioned this wording was added to the law of custody in 1986. The article is not sanctioned. It is likely that it has worked. At the beginning of the 1970's a research study (Kyng, 1974) showed that 85% of children below 1 year were corporally punished. A later study concerning attitudes to children (Varming, 1988) showed that about 40% of the parents used and accepted violence in child rearing. Before § 2,2 came into force an intense professional and public discussion had taken place. The arguments pro were: - that punishment is an inappropriate means of child rearing, that violence begets violence, that violence is forbidden in all other contexts, that children should have rights in this area similar to the adults. The anti-arguments were: - children need limits for their behaviour, society should not intervene in families' internal affairs, that any child would respect punishment from a loving parent, that there was a risk that corporal punishment could be replaced by psychological terror (Goll/Harder, 1986). Sexual assaults were not mentioned in the debate.

Bistandsloven (Law of Social Security): The social needs of families and children are included in the general Bistandsloven concerning almost all social needs. The following summary is chosen as most important regarding the protection of children:

The social security system offers counselling and guidance to any citizen. You can claim anonymity (§28). This is also valid for children and with no minimum age-limit.

The municipal council has the obligation to supervise all children below 18 years (§32).

When children are affected by troubles in the family the social system can offer an (in principle) endless line of different types of support. Economic support, practical support, daycare-institutions, a pedagog (special Danish education) in the home to assist with child upbringing etc. These possibilities are voluntary (§33). Only if the child lives under very unfortunate circumstances and it can be foreseen that its physical development and/or mind might be damaged, is it possible for the public system to intervene without the family's permission (§35). Children have the right to express their opinion as to suggested arrangements if they are 12 years old. If younger they might be asked their opinion. At 15 years old they will, in the Bistandsloven, be regarded as if they were adults, i.e. regarding compulsory placements, children of at least 15 years have the right to a lawyer, to have access to their files, to obtain the reasons for the possible placement outside home, like the rights of their parents.

Before a decision to place a child outside home, a "plan of action" (§66b) has to be drawn up, including the purpose, the duration, special needs of the children, and support to the family during the child's placement.

In Denmark children are placed outside their homes without the parents's wish and will by a political/administrative procedure. A special committee (børn- og ungeudvalget) in every municipality of Denmark, consisting of three politicians, a judge and an expert in pedagogy and psychology decides in this kind of situation. The parents and the child (depending on age) can participate and so can their lawyers and possible observers. The decisions can be appealed to Den sociale Ankestyrelse (the Board of Social Appeals) and thereafter to the Landsretten (High Court).

All citizens have an obligation to inform the municipal council of children who are neglected or degraded by their parents (or any other caretaker) or are living under conditions threatening their health or development (§20). An offence against this article can be punished. Another article (§19) emphasizes the public staff's obligation to react by presumption to social needs.

In line with the fact that professional staff in the field of child care had difficulties handling intervention in families with troubles, a cross-ministerial **document** was published in November 1995. The cooperation between the parents and the system had been particularly criticised. There is a fine line between providing an offer of assistance and the use of force. Between contact and support for a family and control. From a focus on the family unit to a suffering child. The balance in the relationship between the parents and the system alters easily because this is a very vulnerable area. It doesn't take much for the system to be seen as an enemy (by the family). And furthermore there are strong cultural and personal barriers in Denmark against intervention with force. The family is looked upon as a private base where you have the right to be yourself without public intervention (Harder/Mehlbye, 1994).

The above mentioned document concerns assistance to children and youngsters through dialogue and cooperation with the parents. The document is the general official view of how to take care of families in trouble. It is highly detailed with a lot of examples. The first sentence is: "We are all responsible for the children we meet". The major message in the document is to emphasize the specific responsibility for professional staff, especially visiting nurses (who visit 0-year old children on an average of 8 visits per year - and older children when needed), the pedagogical staff in daycare institutions for younger as well as older children, teachers and social workers in social service offices. Another major message is that dialogue and cooperation with parents is central. The obligations and guidelines to act are detailed as to intervention, treatment, juridical aspects etc. The symptoms and signals of children at risk are described. It is emphasized that observation of the signals without interpretation is central. The need for cross-professional cooperation is underlined. Establishment of cross-professional groups in each municipality is required to ensure any child's development, health and growth, since unity and continuity in children's lives are essential. The obligations of the cross-professional groups are detailed in guidance from the Health Board (Sundhedsstyrelsen) based upon a law which came into force January 1996. The guidance also describes a series of children's problems which might lead one to assume special needs.

The Penal Act: The chapter on "Crimes in families" deals with intercourse and surrogate for intercourse as well as neglect and other degrading treatment. The chapter on "Crimes against sexual morality" deals with non-consanguineous sexual crimes and the chapter on "Crimes against Life and Body" is concerned with violence and abuse. As earlier mentioned parents are not expected to use violence in child rearing.

Children and parents at risk

In order to examine children's conditions the State appointed late in the 1980's Det Tværministerielle Børneudvalg (a committee representing 16 ministries with a duty to create unity and coherence in children's lives). This committee initiated a report (Jørgensen et al, 1993) stating that the majority of children in Denmark had good or very good conditions with a high degree of life quality. But a large minority (estimated 15%) did (and does) not share these conditions. The report worked with a tripartition of children at risk:

1. Children with special needs (the size of this group is not defined in the report). This group consists of children suffering from psycho/social stress (defined as for instance illness or death in the family, divorce, unemployment etc.) which they are not able to cope with, at least for the time being. Some of these children will overcome the period of stress via environmental assistance, perhaps including some professional help. The children who are not overcoming their difficulties are:

2. Threatened children. They have been exposed to severe stress but the damage has not yet necessarily become a permanent part of the childrens' personality. They might appear as children with problems in adapting and thriving generally. An estimate of the size of this group is 5%. Professional assistance to the children at an early stage is supposed to change their development in a positive direction.

3. Children with severe problems. These children have early in their lives, and massively, been exposed to very severe stress. Some of the group are estimated to be permanently marginalized and their personality permanently marked. Professional treatment over a long period is necessary to change development. The size of this group is estimated to be about 4%. It is likely that group 3 first and foremost consists of abused and neglected children.

(Thus the first nationwide report on the extent of child abuse and neglect (Christensen, 1992) concerning children between 0-3 years concluded that 10% of all children had unfulfilled social needs and at least 4% were abused (passive or active, physically or psychologically). It was also discovered that 20% of the families were not recognized by society as families with problems.

Estimates of the extent of sexual abuse depend on the definition used. When defined according to the Penal Act i.e. intercourse or surrogate for intercourse, Danish and other Nordic findings vary from 1% to 5% (Nielsen, 1991)).

Presumably, many of the children in group 1 will never be seen as at risk. It is likely that they could be members of any family with occasional problems.

As to the children in groups 2 and 3 they will hopefully be noticed as in trouble and get the necessary assistance. But recognition of children at risk implies that the children or parents have symptoms of, or are signalling, their problems. Furthermore, that the symptoms/signals are perceived by the environment. An extensive study (Dalgaard, unpublished) on physical abuse in Aarhus showed that the parents, often years before the abuse, had signalled their troubles, but were not heard. A newer study (Christoffersen, 1993) found out, through interviews of youngsters earlier placed outside their homes, that rather many of them (previous to the placement) had asked for assistance without result. There are strong cultural, institutional and personal barriers against recognizing families in distress.

So, at the time of recognizing children in severe trouble, the situation has often developed over time. The difficulties have often piled up. The stress on the family members is growing. The network resources might have been mobilized without effective results. Crisis reactions appear. As will be seen from a later passage concerning child protection laws, almost any kind of assistance to families is possible. Placement outside the home is supposed to be chosen only when other types of intervention have been ineffective. Placed childrens' parents (often single) are generally characterized by: Lack of network, unemployment, internal conflicts, drug or alchohol abuse, dependency on welfare payments. They are described as lacking in self-consciousness; they might have mental or psychological problems. The families will often be well known to the social services.

It is difficult to find any significant difference between parents who have accepted their child's placement outside home and those who have not. A possible difference could be the severity of the parents' psychological problems which might mean that voluntary arrangements are difficult to make.

It is certainly likely that parents with many socio-emotional problems have great difficulties in rearing their children. But it is also likely that children lacking visible social and economic problems can be difficult to recognize as neglected or abused children.

Prevention, intervention, treatment and results

Prevention is a code word of the social law. On a **primary prevention level** the Government has for some years initiated special efforts to improve the conditions for children at risk. The intention was to counteract the tendency towards childrens' isolation. The main goals were: Strengthening of cross-professional and cross-sectoral working; anonymous places for counselling of children and youngsters; day- and evening-places for children; improvement in the support for the most vulnerable children using daycare; the schools' role as a social network; improve-ment in the conditions for children of drug and alchohol-abusing parents; focus on second generation of immigrants; revision of the health prevention programme; development of better methods and increase in research. Furthermore, all youngsters after having finished school should have access to further education or work. The plan has consequently been followed up at the primary prevention level by new laws and also by considerable economic support.

On a **secondary prevention level** some communities have been appointed as experimental areas for development of theories and methods. Other communities have the possibility to apply for money for projects with the same goal. And all communities are obliged to establish cross-professional groups to take care of the childrens' conditions in the local area. Further, the Social Ministry has asked experts to write textbooks specifically for the education of social staff (to be finished by the end of 1998) (Socialministeriet, 1996).

The problems in child care as the writer of this chapter sees them are on the **third prevention level**, i.e. intervention in the family and treatment. Over a long period Denmark has, as have many other European countries, been occupied with social de-institutionalization. The purpose has partly been professional as total institutions create rather many problems for those who have to use them, for instance old people and mentally and psychologically disabled persons, and partly economic as total institutions are certainly expensive. This development has also influenced the 24-hour care institutions for children. Many of the bigger institutions have been abolished and were intended to be replaced by more extensive assistance within families. Many treatment places for the whole family, opened only on working days and with various therapeutic backgrounds, were also supposed to replace childrens' placement in institutions. There is no doubt that many families have profited by this, but some parents will not be able to take better care of their children using these types of support.

The social reality is that professional staff have difficulties in finding placements for children in need of placement outside their homes. Some children are put on a waiting-list and some have been returned to their homes because of local lack of money. The possibilities of using professional foster families are diminishing because of the child care institutions' actual need for pedagogues, social workers and psychologists. The consequence has been that many small private institutions have appeared. Even if they can only be established after agreement with the public authorities, they are still private and thus represent a deviation from the Danish tradition of public institutions. The public supervision of these institutions is at a modest level.

Another obvious and worrying problem is that it is difficult to argue that placed children are assisted in a convincing way. Previously placed children have, as adults, significantly greater difficulties than other youngsters of the same age (Christoffersen, 1993) referring to education, job, psychological problems, suicides and suicide-attempts, crime, bonding etc. Maintenance of the relationship to the biological parents was extremely difficult especially for children in foster families. A rather high percentage of the children (now 25 years old) lost contact with biological as well as their foster parents. Placement alone can hardly be the only factor to explain the problems. It is rather a combination of a difficult childhood and a process of often several placements which creates integrational difficulties. However, it is obvious that society has not succeeded in changing the possibilites available to marginalized children in a radical way.

Furthermore, the childrens' parents are beginning to make protests against the fact that their children are being placed outside home as well as against the way the parents are treated during the process by social services. As you will see from the passage concerning the social law, families in troubles are receiving propositions, offers, economic support etc. until a point is reached where the social services estimate that the child's development is as serious risk. At that point the process changes radically; it becomes formal because of the special rules operating in that situation. Compulsory intervention calls for juridical thinking. In the mind of the social worker this has to entail a different relationship to the parents. She has up to that point been a collaborator but will now be seen as a an adversary, by the parents (and perhaps the child) and often also by herself. It is difficult to cross the barrier from voluntary to compulsory intervention. It is also difficult culturally to accept that the parents are not sufficient caretakers for the child. It is likely that the situation calls for the social worker's psychological withdrawal from the parents - which the latter perceive as coldness, bad treatment, disloyalty.

The parents' protests have resulted in establishment of several private associations. The associations represent a wide range of political points of view on the problem of placing children outside their homes (Harder, 1997). They all have fair treatment for the families as a main goal. The associatons have undoubtedly influenced the social perception of the problem whatever their potential radicalism.

Perspectives on the future
As is clear from the previous passages, Denmark is aware of the obvious problems endured by a significant proportion of children and their parents. It will also be clear that there is an awareness of the inefficiency of earlier interventions. There has been an opening made for new ways and new methods. The actual questions are: which way and which methods?

The central problem is a marginalised group of families in need of special assistance to ensure their childrens' development and, at least, to counteract the parents' social deterioration. The method until now has been to intervene, from society's view, with the best intentions but obviously this has also been perceived by many families as a way of disempowering them. The challenge is: how can children be protected against maltreatment without disempowering families? A theme for the future at the Social Ministry's May 1996 conference was integration of marginalised groups. Another theme was solidarity, at a state level, but also between social workers (and other professions) and marginalised groups in order to (re)establish the families' selfconfidence and selfconsciousness. Thoughts about making parents with resources co-responsible for a local area's children were mentioned.

All this calls for a reconsideration of the structure in Denmark regarding attitudes, solidarity and economy. And for a change in the paradigm of social work. You may have some doubts as to how far this can be attained. Social work has always been in a process of change in relation to social structure, social policy etc. The main purpose has first and foremost been to adapt the client to society's actual demands and expectations. Social work is characterized by dilemmas. The social worker is expected to assist people with social problems, a process which includes the establishment of an emotional contact. But she is also expected to reach visible results. When social work involvement concerns child abuse and neglect the families (at least those we know) will often be underprivileged and marginalised across generations. They will therefore often have generational experience of society's (mal)treatment of them. This will create opposition against the authorities. Gustav Jonsson (1969) called, in the 1960's, these families "quilled". This expression is not only true for the 1960's. Jonsson emphasized the necessity of establishing a true interaction between the family and the social worker. Only through the social worker's constant maintenance of an equal relationship, could the family develop enough confidence to be more open and less shameful. This takes time - what has been created through generations cannot be changed rapidly. It is necessary to think in a generational way about prevention. The social worker has to be prepared to receive perhaps several generations' feelings, also (and maybe especially) anger. Jonsson's work in several ways was similar to newer empowerment theories. He had great impact on Danish social work in the 1960's and 1970's, i.e. in a period of prosperity and much better conditions for social work than today. But, as will already be clear, the problems are not yet solved.

The way forward is not easy to choose.

One way could be early placement of children at risk. Denmark places most children relatively late in their childhood in contradiction to other Nordic countries which also tend to use compulsory adoption. This would comply with the child's need for continuity during childhood. There are obvious problems: how will it be possible to judge which parents through social work assessment could be good or acceptable parents for their children? We are only at a preliminary stage of (perhaps) being able to judge and operationalize parental abilities. And the judgement has to be prospective. Ethically this calls for a series of considerations: Who can judge? According to which standard? Can a massive social intervention change the situation? When? Etc. And this solution also calls for a withdrawal from the cultural perception of the family as the natural home for the child.

Another way is to focus on the whole family with all possible support to all members. As described earlier in this section, this way has until now not been sufficiently successful.

A third way is, as mentioned, to focus on the local area as responsible for all the area's children. This should include a professional staff, the citizens of the area, self-help groups etc. It might be a new way even if it is also a kind of return to local caretaking of an earlier time. The third way has been (and is) tried with marginalised groups (for instance in the earlier mentioned SUM-programme). As the evaluation of this programme showed (Adamsen/Fisker 1993), many projects were effective in getting in contact with individuals and families who did not earlier make use of the local possibilities and resources. But one specific group was never "caught": the extremely marginalised individuals and families; not even when they were included in the remit of the project.

A **future way** has to include:
- changing the attitudes of society to marginalized families.
Whilst structural development tends towards growing individualization which promotes distant attitudes towards disadvantaged people, there is obviously another trend, represented by the Social Ministry as well as voluntary assistance to groups with social needs.
Denmark has a tradition of solidarity at a state level (the welfare society). Because of the ongoing debate about the extent of the welfare state, the Social Research Institute recently made a survey on public attitudes to it (Socialforsknings-instituttet, 1996). The report shows an ambivalence. On one hand there is a massive support for society's obligations towards "weak groups" (yet with some differentiation between self-inflicted or not self-inflicted situations). On the other hand, the welfare society is perceived as too extended and too expensive. So society has a deep engagement in securing state level solidarity with an emphasis on groups in need.
At the same time, a high percentage of the population use their personal surplus in voluntary work, i.e. personal solidarity.
Changes in attitudes to human beings with psychological diseases are the subject of an actual health ministry project. Experiences from the project could be transferred to the area of marginalized families.

Public engagement in securing the welfare of groups in need and the Social Ministry's engagement with marginalized groups, amongst them children and their parents, might contain a contradiction. On one hand the groups are accepted as in need of societal assistance, on the other hand a special attention to the marginalized families might contribute to the families' feeling of extended societal control. It is certainly necessary that the Social Ministry's and the Health Board's demands concerning dialogue with the families should be reflected in social practice to avoid a further marginalization of families. Use of family conferences based on experiences from New Zealand (Sandbek/Tveiten 1996) might (re)establish the families' feeling of being able to influence their situation.

Furthermore, a future way has to include:
- involvement of the local area.

Roughly, there are two groups of children and parents (which are known to the social services as families with problems). One group consists of children in distress but with parents in at least some dialogue and cooperation with the local social services. This group is often a marginalized group. The other group are families experiencing a collision between the interests of the children and the parents. The latter is the smallest category but also the group with the most severe problems. This group is extremely marginalized, perhaps outcast families.

Solidarity and assistance from the local area will likely be most successful for the first group. The local area includes the professional staff and the inhabitants. Increased attention, early intervention and support could improve the conditions of children and parents. The Social Ministry's previously mentioned guidance and the development in relation to local projects is supporting this approach.

As to the other group: families with severe problems, it is much more difficult for the local area to support them. These families have for generations been very challenging to the social system. The children will often be unable to stay at home. Support from the local area could mean establishment in the local area of small institutions for the children when needed. This might ensure maintenance of contact between the local authorities and the parents, between the local authorities and the child, between the child and the parents. Contact between the institution and the local area through common activities could improve the child's integration in the local society. A local institution also provides the possibility of grouping more parents in order to strengthen their perception of themselves and their possibilities for action.

This also calls for

- changed conditions for social work.

Administration and bureaucracy have a restrictive influence on intensive and creative support and treatment of children and parents. Juridical thinking has to some extent to be replaced by developmental thinking.

And for

- a change of the social workers' (and other professional staff's) attitudes to extremely marginalized children and parents. As mentioned before in this chapter, parents are questioning the social workers' communication with, and attitudes to, them. Social research has for some years explored this area through interviews with parents. The results seem concordant. Parents who did not feel that they were helped saw the reasons as: different perceptions of necessary assistance, unacceptable or non-accessible assistance or classification of the problem without further intervention. Families who felt that they were assisted were met on their level of acknowledgement of the problems, they were heard and they got sufficient time (Christensen, 1991). Uggerhøj (1994) expresses the parents' wishes to the social worker as: humanity, engagement and fairness. The previously mentioned private organizations for families in distress also underline this. And, at the May 1995-conference the social minister in her introduction recommended that social workers and similar staff, in their contact with families, should combine the old conception of "vocation" (known within social work from the very beginning and before professionalization) with professional consciousness. Still, it has to be remembered that the relationship between the social worker and the family in distress is asymetric. The social worker is representing society's values and demands and the family's powerlessness cannot be removed only by fair and empathic treatment even if it might strenghten the family's respect for itself. As Habermas underlines (Dahlberg-Larsen, 1994), the world of systems tends to colonialize the world of private life especially in the social welfare area. The result might be powerless and alienated human beings. The social worker constantly has to be aware of the difficult task and to counteract these effects. This is a constant ethical challenge. And also a challenge for the institutions of social education.

Notes

1) Frode Muldkjær is now chairman of the Børnerådet (The Children's Board) which is an experimental project initiated by the Government. The purpose is to give children possibilities of influencing the development, and the Board is in constant dialogue with children all over Denmark.

2) The writer of this chapter was and is still a member of the prevention group in Northern Jutland.

3) More than 300 people from the five Nordic countries participated in the first Nordic seminar on Child Abuse and Neglect. The number of participants are still growing.

References

Adamsen, L./Fisker, J.: "Socialt forsøgsarbejde i boligområder", AKF's Forlag 1986.

Andersen, B.H.: "Anbringelsesforløb - en registerundersøgelse af børn og unge anbragt uden for hjemmet", rapport 89:2, Socialforskningsinstituttet 1989.

Backe, L. et al: "Incest - en bog om blodskam", Reitzel 1983.

Betænkning om de retlige rammer for indsatsen over for børn og unge, Afgivet af udvalget om de retlige rammer for indsatsen over for børn og unge. Betænkning nr. 1212, 1990.

"Borgerne om velfærdssamfundet", ed. by Jørgen Søndergaard, Socialforskningsinstituttet 1996.

Børnekommissionens betænkning nr. 918, København 1981.

"Børnemishandling i Norden", ed. by Merrick, J., Reitzel 1985.

"Børne- og ungdomsforskning - tendenser og perspektiver", ed. by Bøgh, C./Parkvig, K., Socialstyrelsens Informations- og Konsulentvirksomhed (SIKON), 1989.

Christensen, E.: "Trængte familier", rapport 91:8, Socialforskningsinstituttet, 1991.

Christensen, E.: "Omsorgssvigt? - en rapport om de 0-3-årige baseret på sundhedsplejerskers viden", rapport 92:7, Socialforskningsinstituttet 1992.

Christoffersen, M.N.: "Anbragte børns livsforløb", rapport 93:11, Socialforskningsinstituttet 1993.

Dahlberg-Larsen, J.: "Lovene og livet", Akademisk Forlag 1994.

Dalgaard, L.: unpublished.

Davis, I.P.: "Socialrådgivning - teori og metodik", Danmarks Sociale Højskole 1964.

Ertmann, B.: "Tvangsfjernelser - en analyse af samtlige tvangsfjernelser i Københavns kommune 1990", Kroghs Forlag A/S, 1994.

Goll, A.: "Udvalgte skrifter", Munksgaard 1940.

Goll, O.: "Grunduddannelseskvalitetsprojektet GUK - forprojektet", 1990.

Goll, O./Harder, M.: "Handling eller mishandling? - forebyggelse af - og indgriben i - mishandling af børn", Aalborg Universitetsforlag 1986.

Harder, M./Mehlbye, J.: "Barrièrer for identifikation og indgriben" in "Overgreb mod børn - ser vi det? gør vi noget?", Det kriminalpræventive Råd 1994.

Harder, M.: "Samfundsmagt - Forældremodstand - foreninger til støtte for familier med anbragte børn", Aalborg Universitetsforlag 1997.

Horsten, H.: "Børne- og Ungdomsforsorgen i Danmark", Nyt Nordisk Forlag Arnold Busck 1970.

Jonsson, G.: "Det sociale arvet", Tidens Forlag Stockholm, 1969.

Jørgensen, P.S. et al: "Kommunernes børnesager - en undersøgelse af forebyggelse, visitation og anbringelser i syv kommuner", rapport 89:1, Socialforskningsinstituttet 1989.

Jørgensen, P.S. et al: "Risikobørn - hvem er de? - hvad gør vi?", Socialministeriet/Det tværministerielle Børneudvalg, 1993.

Kampmann, P./Nielsen, Nielsen, F.v.N.: "Tal om børn", Det tværministerielle Børneudvalg 1995

Kempe, C. H./Helfer, R.E.: "The Battered Child", University of Chicago Press 1968.

Kopart, H.H./Sørensen, I.M.L.: "Børnemishandling", Demos 1977.

Kyng, B.: "Opvækstvilkår og udvikling", Gyldendals Pædagogiske Bibliotek 1974.

Larsen, F.W./Ydebo,I: "Anbringelse uden for hjemmet", Ugeskrift for Læger, p. 7542, 1994.

Lingås, L.G.: "Hva kan vi lære av tysk sosialt arbeid?" in Bader, K.: "Hjælpeløse hjælpere", Reitzel 1993.

Løkke, A.: "Vildfarende børn", Socpol 1989.

Nielsen, B.G.: "Seksuelle overgreb mod børn i familien - et offerperspektiv på straffesystemet", Aarhus Universitetsforlag 1991.

Sandbek, M./Tveiten, G.: "Sammen med familien - Arbeid i partnerskab med barn og familier", Kommuneforlaget, 1996.

Sigsgaard, E.: "Om børn og deres virkelighed - set i perioder over 300 år", Reitzel 1982.

Skytte, M.: "Etniske minoritetsfamilier og socialt arbejde", Reitzel 1997

Socialministeriet: "Nye veje i indsatsen - rapport fra konference om indsatsen over for de svagest stillede børn, unge og børnefamilier", Juni 1996.

Sundhedsstyrelsens retningslinier, Forebyggende sundhedsordninger for børn og unge (based on law 438 of 14.6.1995).

Uggerhøj, L.: "Hjælp eller afhængighed", Aalborg Universitets Forlag 1995.

Varming, O.: "Holdninger til børn", Gyldendal 1988.

Ydebo, I.: "Hjælpeforanstaltninger for børn og unge på grund af velfærdstrussel, Lovgivningens baggrund og udvikling samt emnets omfang i København belyst ud fra en analyse af Børne- og Ungdomsnævnets virksomhed i 1983, Del I: 1988.

Child Protection in England and Wales

By Keith Pringle

Introduction

I would like to make two preliminary remarks about the material in this chapter. My first preliminary remark relates to the topic I am addressing here. For on the whole I confine my analysis to protection of children within England and Wales: Scotland has different procedures for dealing with child abuse and indeed the welfare of children more generally (Lister 1995).

My second remark is about the format of this chapter. It is divided into three sections. The first surveys the development of services for the protection of children up until the 1970s. The second looks at the concept of "Child Protection" that developed in Britain from the mid-1970s and which, until at least recently, dominated child welfare services in this country. The last section, entitled "The Way Forward?", considers possible future developments.

The protection of children up to 1970s

Many of the same dilemmas about how to protect children recur across the modern history of child abuse in Britain: punishment or care for abusers; removal or rehabilitation of abused children; focus of services on the child or the abuser; ambivalent attitudes to mothers of abused children. Of course neither the welfare of children nor child abuse are recent phenomena, although the social construction of both has changed over time.

Considerable debate exists about the status of childhood in medieval times both in Britain and elsewhere, largely due to lack of reliable data or its uneven spread in terms of class, locality and culture (see Aries 1985 and Frost and Stein 1989 Chapter 2 for critiques of Aries' work). Nevertheless, it seems that in the England of the Middle Ages a relatively effective community response may have existed to the destitution of children (Frost and Stein 1989).

Similar uncertainty exists around the relatively more modern history of child abuse (Pollock 1983). What seems clear is that although child abuse was socially condemned from at least the end of the eighteenth century in England, mounting concern about it is particularly apparent in the last three decades of the nineteenth.

By 1889 a specific charity, the National Society for the Prevention of Cruelty to Children (NSPCC), had formed out of earlier local societies. In that same year the British Parliament instituted the very first Prevention of Cruelty to Children Act (followed by another soon after in 1894), providing statutory powers for protection of children carried out by the inspectors of the NSPCC in conjunction with the police.

In Britain, Harry Ferguson has made a particularly revealing study of the NSPCC in the period from the 1880s to 1914 (Ferguson 1990, 1992) paralleling the equally striking work of Linda Gordon in the United States (Gordon 1989). His research makes several important points. One is that the approach of the NSPCC changed quite markedly in a short period of time from an emphasis on punishment of abusers and removal of children to one of moral improvement of abusers and potential rehabilitation of children with families (Ferguson 1990). As we shall see later in this chapter, a similar debate between these two approaches has been played out in the more recent history of child welfare in Britain.

Ferguson also demonstrates conclusively that child maltreatment at the end of the nineteenth century was a clearly identified social problem in terms of physical assaults, incest and neglect on the part of parents (1990, 1992). However, it was viewed by those taking an interest in it at the time as a phenomenon of the lower orders. And, even then, child abuse was seen as characteristic of only a certain portion of those lower orders: the "undeserving poor" - regarded as dangerous and/or morally inadequate. Here, once again in embryonic form, is a central motif which runs throughout debates about the protection of children in Britain over the next century: is child abuse the product of a dangerous and identifiable minority within the population - or a manifestation of some more general malaise within society? The answer to this question for most philanthropists and NSPCC inspectors in late nineteenth century Britain was relatively clear. On the whole the problem was seen as residing in particular individuals rather than the structures of the society where they lived.

Moreover, child abuse does not at that time seem to have been linked to the Victorian middle class family norm of physical chastisement of children; nor to the institutionalised physical abuse of some public school traditions [Note for readers outside the UK: in Britain "public school" actually means a privately financed school - at the end of the nineteenth century these were the exclusive preserve of the ruling classes].

Certainly no connection was made between the "depraved" sexual behaviour which was publically recognised as existing in some lower class families and sexual assaults on children which we now know occurred in the homes of the middle or upper classes and in the public schools. These assaults were not publically recognised and our evidence for them derives largely from "post hoc" anecdotal and historical evidence: for instance the now infamous, but then seriously hidden, sexual abuse of Virginia Woolf as a child by her step-brother, George Duckworth (Bell 1976).

So at the end of the nineteenth century in Britain child abuse was socially constructed as a significant problem but one which related to specific sections of the lower orders. The reasons for this particular social construction are debatable and, to an extent, unfathomable. It may be linked to a contemporary awareness of the need for limited social welfare measures to counter the effects of the destruction of rural communities as a result of land enclosures linked with that rapid urbanisation in the nineteenth century which made Britain the first industrialised society of the modern era. There is no doubt that this demand for "welfare" was largely a product of the need to maintain a regularly competent industrial workforce (Clarke 1993). However, the welfare impetus seems to have grown stronger as the nineteenth century progressed and it is important to think about why this should be so.

Some commentators place an emphasis on the growth of urban and industrial unrest consequent upon the economic cycles of capitalism and particularly the "Great Depression" which developed in the 1880s (Frost and Stein 1989). Nor should we discount the impact at that time of ideas based on Social Darwinism. Such concerns about racial purity gained wide currency in late nineteenth century Britain partly due to the perceived threat to Britain's economic and military predominance from the new German empire. That context at this time was also set by Britain's military humiliation at the hands of the South African Boers. Even the reforming rationale developed by prominent welfare proponents such as the socialists Beatrice and Sidney Webb partly derived from Social Darwinist perspectives and the idea that social measures contributed to a strategy for the preservation of an imperial "race" (Rich 1990, Saggar 1992).

This was at least part of the framework within which measures for the protection of children developed with considerable rapidity around the turn of the new century. They culminated in the 1908 Children Act, consolidating provisions against child abuse, and the the Poor Law Institutions Order of 1913 which moved children between the ages of three and sixteen years out of the "workhouses" and into child-specific institutions.

However, we need to place such measures in perspective. The legislation to protect children was still relatively minimalist and achieved only against considerable resistance in Parliament. The nature of this resistance is important in helping us to understand future history, and is well-illustrated in this contemporary view from Lord Shaftesbury delivered in a parliamentary debate at the time (Frost and Stein 1989 p.45): "The evils you state are enormous and indisputable but they are of so private, internal and domestic a character as to be beyond the reach of legislation...". Only in the face of potential revolution and/or imminent imperial decline could such intervention be accepted, and even then only in minimalist fashion.

A common saying even now in Britain is that "An englishMAN's home is his castle" - and this concept of family privacy is one which has recurrently entered into all British debates on protection of children (and indeed social welfare more generally) up to and including the present day. Moreover, my emphasis on "MAN" in "englishman" is important in this context. As Cannan (1992 p.55) notes, the limited welfare reforms at the end of the nineteenth century in relation to men, women and children were carefully designed as far as possible not to undermine what was seen as the legitimate authority of men in their families. So when we speak of "family privacy" what we are really referring to is the assumed right of men to privacy within the domestic sphere. This tension between the right of men to domestic privacy on the one hand and, on the other, the right of children to safety in the home is a further theme which runs through debates on the protection of children over the next century. However, the largely gendered quality of this tension has been (and still is) disguised by commentators referring to the rights of parents conflicting with the rights of children: i.e. they use terminology which is ungendered.

Placing these issues in a European context, it seems to me that it is impossible to over-rate the cultural importance of individualism and the privacy of the family in the history of social welfare in Britain. In a recent comparison of child protection in France and Britain (Cooper et al. 1995 pp.18-19, 98-101), the authors note that:

"Child protection practices cannot but reflect and be shaped by the wider society of which they are a part, although they also help to reproduce that broader social and political context. Contemporary English society is powerfully shaped by ideologies of political and social individualism. By contrast, French society since the revolution of 1789 and the creation of the first Republic is firmly rooted in collectivist principles" (p. 18).

And later, they add:

"In British child care law the individual and the state are potential adversaries whose interests are effectively irreconcilable. It is for these reasons that Britain has no explicit 'family policy'...[T]he inevitable effect of [Britain's] non-interventionist stance is to identify, by default, those 'against' whom the state must intervene as pathetic and pathological" (p. 100).

So it was in 1897 and, as we shall see later, so it still is in 1997.

In the period between 1918 and 1939 the issue of child abuse generally became less prominent. On the other hand, the NSPCC consolidated its machinery in relation to physical abuse and neglect while child welfare legislation was further codified, particularly in the Children and Young Person's Act 1933. However, it is highly significant that one form of child abuse, which was acknowledged at the end of the nineteenth century, virtually disappeared without trace at this time: sexual abuse. It might be worth readers considering why that particular form of abuse disappeared from public recognition - and why, indeed, it was only rediscovered in Britain in the 1980s. We shall return to that important question later in the chapter. For the time being let us concentrate on what happened to protection of children from physical abuse and neglect in England and Wales after 1945.

With hindsight it may be that we should regard the social and political climate of 1945 as an aberration in the long-term social welfare trajectory of Britain, albeit an aberration which dictated the shape of the country's welfare system for the next quarter century. We noted above that English society (unlike its counterpart in much of continental Europe) seems to have a long and deeply-rooted commitment to individualism at the expense of notions such as solidarity or social inclusion (Adams 1996). In a sense, the period 1945-1970 in Britain is an exception to this rule and thereby stands out both from what went before and what happened later. At the end of the Second World War in 1945, the population of Britain almost immediately elected out of office the war hero Churchill and into office the Labour leader Clement Attlee. The latter had a mandate to institute a welfare system which would reflect the intense feelings of social solidarity promoted by the extreme privations of the 1930s and the War, as well as the euphoria arising from recent victory (Frost and Stein 1989 p.33).

Two additional factors at this time were also important in determining the next stage of child welfare policy. The first was the professional background of Attlee. At one time he had been a social administration academic and in the mid 1930s published an important text entitled "The Social Worker" (Cooper et al. 1995 p.101). This book already made clear his commitment to social work as a key profession in working with families and in the process of dealing with newly identified social need. The second factor was the death in foster care of a child named Denis O'Neill. The public concern aroused by this tragedy partly fuelled a movement which led in 1948 to a new reforming Children Act and the setting up of discrete Children's Departments around the country with a specific brief to promote the protection and welfare of children. In many ways these Children's Departments were the direct ancestors of the Social Services Departments which are still at the heart of the current child welfare system in England and Wales. Moreover, the child care workers in those departments were the direct ancestors of today's social workers. Indeed, when I first trained as a social worker in 1979 the law I was operating was that same 1948 Children Act.

In passing we should note that policy changes driven by a public scandal surrounding the death or abuse of children is another recurrent theme in the post-war history of British child welfare (Reder et al. 1993). We shall meet this phenomenon repeatedly later in the chapter. The reaction to the death of Denis O' Neill was the "prototype" for those cases that have followed in its wake.

The socialist Government of 1945 in a series of measures (of which the 1948 Children Act was one) constructed what became known as the "Welfare State". It is important not to idealise this structure: it had many inherent flaws and was the product of numerous compromises (Clarke and Langan 1993). Nevertheless, in some ways the "Welfare State" represented a massive break with the past and an equally massive leap forward in terms of British acceptance of the expanded boundaries of social welfare (Frost and Stein 1989).

With regard to child welfare, these changes were important not only for the implementation of new structures which we have already noted but also for the new philosophies which underpinned the practice of the Children's Officers and their staff. At least on the surface the moral endeavour of the philanthropist was abandoned, to be replaced by the new "professional" social work technologies of psychodynamics and social casework, based on models developed in New Deal America (Lorenz 1995).

Some commentators (Frost and Stein 1989) suggest that the new ethos of social welfare which dominated practice in the 1950s and the 1960s can be directly linked to the post-war political climate of consensus which characterised both Labour and Conservative governments throughout those decades. Whether that is true or not, there certainly was a new welfare ethos which had some distinct features very relevant to our account.

One feature was a greater commitment to universal provision of services than had hitherto been the case in Britain: the division between the deserving and undeserving poor, so entrenched in previous British welfare ideology and practice, became to some extent less marked. This phenomenon was reflected most clearly in the form of some universal monetary benefits. However, it also manifested itself, perhaps less obviously, in the approach of the new welfare professionals in the Children's Departments. Armed with the humanist/psychodynamic frameworks of american social work academics such as Perlman (1957), Biestek (1961) and Hollis (1964), as well the dominant concept of maternal deprivation developed by John Bowlby (1953), British child care social workers of the 1950s and the 1960s tended to break down the barriers between child abuse and child care. The former came to be regarded as a manifestation of a poor experience of the latter. Parents who physically abused or neglected their children were seen as themselves being the pathological outcomes of their own negative childhood experiences. The implications of such a perspective were important in terms of our survey.

For, within that perspective, the way to "treat" child abusing parents was primarily to offer them psychological and emotional support. They were to be provided with a new and positive parenting experience, the social worker "re-parenting" the parent, most usually the female parent. Note the issue of gender here. During the Second World War there had been an unprecedented influx of women in to the labour market, assisted by extensive day care provision and temporary fostering of children away from urban centres. After the war, with the return of men to the labour market, the labour participation of women was discouraged. This discouragement was sometimes achieved in very concrete ways such as assumptions about woman-based home-care built into the post-war welfare plans of William Beveridge (Williams 1989 pp.125-8). It was also discouraged by that maternal-deprivation thesis which so dominated child care social work thinking in post-war Britain.

The post-war treatment paradigm for child abuse described above clearly fits into these deeply gendered perspectives: for the mother was the main pathological object of attention, and the person offering professional "nurturance" to her was generally a woman too, since most child care social workers were female. Earlier we noted that gender was an important, though often silent, issue in child welfare reforms at the end of the nineteenth century. In the 1950s and 1960s we again discern its unspoken but critical importance. As we shall see later, gender has also been a vital component of debates around child abuse from the 1980s up to and including the present time. The major difference now is that gender issues are no longer unspoken; though, as we shall also see, there are many forces seeking to silence those discourses which continue to make gender an explicit component of debates about child abuse.

However, let us return to the post-war social work technology of treating abusive parents which is our current concern. We should note two further important and related points about that treatment paradigm. First, it no longer sought to isolate parents who abused their children as dangerous deviants. Rather than being "bad", such parents were now viewed as being either "sad" (i.e. in need of emotional help) or occasionally "mad" (i.e in need of psychiatric or psychological assistance). Instead of being regarded as essentially a criminal act, child abuse increasingly became the domain of the "helping professions": either social workers using pseudo-medical technologies and/or medical personnel, both groups tending to adopt a relatively optimistic approach to the potential outcomes of their systematic procedures for re-parenting parents (Dale et al. 1986).

Second, these perspectives implied optimism not only in terms of treatment outcomes but also in terms of prevention. For the logic of this approach suggested that it should be possible to predict which individuals would become abusive parents, based largely upon their past life experiences and to some extent on their current ones. Herein lies the origin of child abuse risk checklists (Dingwall 1989, Parton and Parton 1989) which became so influential at that time and which, as we shall see, in a somewhat disguised form maintain a pervasive implicit influence on child protection social work to the present day (Pringle 1995 p.45).

There were, of course, many other developments in the post-war welfare world which contributed to the child abuse paradigm I have outlined here. I will mention only two, both of which had a critical importance in Britain.

First the pseudo-medical/medical nature of that paradigm meshed with some very compatible developments occurring in the diagnosis of physical abuse. Partly as a result of radiographic advances in the U.S during the Second World War and the immediate post-war period, it became possible to detect bone fractures far more effectively than hitherto, including harm to young children. From these develop-ments arose Kempe's (1962) influential delineation of a "battered baby syndrome", containing all the hallmarks which we have described above and leading to a re-emergent social awareness of physical abuse as a major problem, but this time as a medical and psychological rather than criminal phenomenon.

Second, some commentators (N. Parton 1985, Cannan 1992 pp. 57-60) suggest that the re-emergence of physical abuse was then taken up by certain welfare professionals in Britain for whom it served a very useful professional and political purpose. Cannan and Parton specifically refer to two groups: paediatricians, whose professional ambit was otherwise being eroded by general improvements occurring in child health; and the NSPCC.

Whatever the precise nature of these interactions, it is clear that over time in the 1950s, 1960s and 1970s issues of child welfare in Britain became increasingly focused on the prevention and treatment of child abuse. In many respects this paradigm, which focused on psychological support for abusing parents rather than punishment and which was based (uncharacteristically for Britain) on a sense of social solidarity, bears some close resemblances with responses to child abuse found at the present time in many countries of western and northern Europe (Davies and Sale 1989, Pringle 1996).

It is probably fair to say that this post-war paradigm of child abuse and child welfare, inscribed in the Children and Young Persons Acts 1963 and 1969, dominated welfare responses until the 1970s and, indeed, well into the 1980s. Significant elements remain central even now in some sections of the "helping professions". Certainly, this was the paradigm within which I was trained as a social worker in the late 1970s and early 1980s. It was also the perspective which to a large extent informed my practice as a newly qualified social worker.

However, during the 1970s several dispararate trends began to develop in terms of economics, politics, culture and ideology which together initiated a long process eroding the certainties of the post-war treatment paradigm. Ultimately, these trends led to a sea-change in child welfare policy and practice and to a new orthodoxy which is only now, in the late 1990s, being itself seriously challenged. It is the development of that new orthodoxy, Child Protection, from the 1970s onwards to which we now turn.

From protecting children to child protection: the late 1970s to the late 1990s in British child welfare policy and practice.

It is difficult to pin-point where the process of erosion of the post-war paradigm began. So I will merely summarise the main forces contributing to that erosion without trying to decide which was the first or most important: anyway in reality they coalesced.

One important background factor was surely the rapidly changing economic climate in Britain from the mid-1970s onwards precipitated by the so-called "oil crisis" (Parton 1991 pp. 204-5, Clarke and Langan 1993). The interaction of this ongoing economic crisis with certain characteristics of the "Welfare State" is a complex story. The critical points in that story are: lower economic growth provided less national resources; higher unemployment had direct and indirect national income and welfare cost implications; an ageing population again implied national income and welfare cost outcomes; inherent weaknesses in the Beveridge post-war welfare scheme were exacerbated by less resources and greater welfare demands. In summary, the material basis of welfare provision established in 1945 was increasingly unworkable.

In terms of responses to child abuse, the implications of this were several-fold. The overall impact was mounting pressure in all welfare services to start targeting resource allocations which ran counter, of course, to the universal-orientation of much post-war provision. In the short-run such a pressure for targeting of resources meant that the application of child abuse risk checklisting, to isolate suitable cases for treatment, became even more urgent. In the longer-term, there was clearly some major conflict between shrinkage of resources on the one hand and, on the other hand, the massive expansion of the child abuse technology which was central to the post-war paradigm. This was especially the case when that technology, based on long-term one-to-one therapeutic assistance to abusing parents, was clearly very labour-intensive and very expensive.

What added further urgency to this conflict between resources and service provision was growing criticism in the 1970s and 1980s, from a variety of different sources, about the ineffectiveness of the post-war paradigm of child abuse treatment (Dale et al. 1986, N. Parton 1985 and 1991 chapter 7, Parton and Parton 1989, Frost and Stein 1989 chapter 7, Cannan 1992 chapter 3, Langan 1993, Pringle 1995 chapter 3). As N. Parton (1991 pp. 193-4) chronicles, a number of parliamentary committees and research studies called into question the effectiveness of professional child care services. One of the most powerful contributions to this ethos of doubt was a catalogue of well-publicised "scandals" centring mainly on enquiries into the deaths of children, often at the hands of their parents or step-parents. In many cases the ensuing public enquiries concluded that these children were insufficiently protected by child welfare services (Cochrane 1993, Reder et al. 1993), beginning with the death of Maria Colwell in 1973 (N. Parton 1985). The obvious question arose: if tragedies like these seemed to be happening so often, what use was the massive and expensive child abuse treatment technology which had grown between 1948 and the mid-1980s? It seems to me that this critique of the post-war treatment paradigm, within which I practised as a social worker, was largely correct. By focusing primarily on support to abusive parents rather than on the immediate protection of children, that paradigm sometimes failed badly.

Assaults on the post-war treatment paradigm also came from other directions. Civil libertarian advocates on both the Right and the Left of politics were critical of the increasing numbers of children entering the care system without what was regarded by those advocates as sufficient due legal process. Particular hostility was directed at the rapidly increasing use of "Place of Safety Orders" for emergency admissions to care; and at "Parental Rights Resolutions" whereby parental rights over children who were in the "voluntary" care of Social Services Departments could be taken by the latter without any recourse to the Courts. These measures managed to offend both campaigners for childrens' rights and those for parents'rights (N. Parton 1991 pp. 196-7).

In the early 1980s further doubt was cast upon the post-war paradigm by powerful critiques of its basic premise about the causes of child abuse. There were two rather different critiques. However, what they had in common was a certainty that explanations of child abuse based exclusively on ideas about individual pathology were no longer tenable. The first critique was essentially left-wing and most clearly represented in the highly influential work of Nigel Parton (1985). His main contention was that an adequate understanding of child abuse was only possible if its social causes were recognised: i.e. the massive stresses of poverty, over-crowding and unemployment which allegedly contributed to some parents harming their children physically and emotionally. Later, his critique focused on the inadequacies of risk checklists which used largely individual criteria (Dingwall 1989, Parton and Parton 1989). This important aspect of the critique demonstrated conclusively that, as precise tools for welfare professionals seeking to prevent physical abuse, such risk checklists were virtually worthless.

The second critique emanated from advocates of a relatively new welfare technology which in the late 1970s and early 1980s had mainly been imported from the United states: family therapy. The most influential British expression of this critique was provided in the work of the Rochdale NSPCC team led by Peter Dale (Dale et al. 1986). Their basic premise was that the post-war paradigm of nurturing pathological individuals had signally failed for two reasons. First, because child abuse had to be understood primarily as a symptom of a dysfunctional family rather than the product of an individual adult with a damaged childhood history. Second, because working with dysfunctional families required a firm, potentially punitive, legal mandate rather than some vague voluntary agreement between "client" and therapist.

Moreover, Dale et al. argued that within this firm legal mandate, focused, relatively short-term family restructuring was required rather than the long-term psychodynamic counselling characteristic of the post-war paradigm. If such clear restructuring failed to produce concrete results within the time-scales set, then the Rochdale team had no hesitation in recommending a more punitive response to secure the safety of the child.

The work of Nigel Parton and Peter Dale has had a major influence on the shape of Government policy and practice in relation to child abuse since the late 1980s. In particular, the imprint of both their critiques can clearly been seen in one of the most important practice documents issued by the Department of Health in the last ten years. "Protecting Children" (Department of Health 1988) is the Government guidance for social workers undertaking assessments in child abuse cases. It is still probably the major influence on most such assessments carried out in this country. We now need to explain why the critiques of Parton and Dale have found such favour with the British Government.

So far we have explained the erosion of the post-war child abuse paradigm in terms of economic pressures, failures in protecting children, civil liberties contraventions and aetiological weakness. As if these were not enough, the paradigm also ran into conflict with another force in some ways more powerful than any other opposing it. That force was political and ideological and found its material expression after the British parliamentary elections of 1979.

In reality, one cannot separate what happened politically in 1979 from some of the other, already pre-existing, factors which we have surveyed: in particular the changing economic climate and the growing problems of the "Welfare State". Nevertheless, it is unlikely that the post-war welfare paradigm would have been so thoroughly dismantled after 1979 without the election as Prime Minister in that year of Margaret Thatcher.

The post-war paradigm of child welfare was an anathema to the philosophy of Thatcherism in many ways. Her concern to destroy what she referred to as the "nanny state" clearly had direct implications for a model of welfare which treated adults abusing their children as people in need of nurturance and re-parenting by officers of the state.

Her insistence that there was no such thing as society flew in the face of a model of welfare predicated on the traditionally un-British concept of social solidarity. And her suspicion of what she regarded as "the enemy within" implied a turning away from the notion that violence was perpetrated by people who were "sad" or "mad": Thatcherism was much more comfortable with the concept of "badness". The arrival of Thatcherism presaged a reinstatement of discrimination between a majority of citizens deemed to be "good" and a troublesome minority judged to be "bad": a return to the deserving and undeserving poor reminiscent of pre-1945 Britain - indeed, reminiscent of the late nineteenth century.

That this was the case was confirmed by Thatcher's overtly stated ambition to restore Britain to "Victorian values", and that included Victorian notions of social welfare. In some (but not all) ways what happened to welfare policies directed at child abuse between 1979 and 1995 was indeed a return to the late nineteenth century.

A central welfare principle arising from this philosophy was the requirement to identify the (allegedly) rather small dangerous minority within society, deal firmly with them, and then withdraw state intervention from the lives of the vast majority of citizens who were deemed to be good and true. Moreover, such a welfare principle worked to the benefit of economic necessity as well as ideological purity. This was especially the case as it implied the costly post-war goals of abuse treatment and abuse prevention could be replaced by the much cheaper target of identifying and dealing with an (allegedly) small number of child abusers.

Clearly, identification of dangerousness required use of some form of child abuse risk checklist. Yet, of course, such checklists had been effectively debunked by the Partons and others (see above). This apparent dilemma for welfare policy makers post-1979 was, however, easily solved. For the critiques of Parton and of Dale did not in fact undercut the essential idea of identifying dangerousness: all those critiques did was change some of the criteria by which dangerousness could be (allegedly) pinpointed. Instead of a crusade to identify dangerous individuals, the search was now on to identify dangerous families (Dale) or dangerous social conditions (Nigel Parton) which in turn became associated with sectors of the working classes.

I should emphasise that this latter association was never intended by Parton himself. It is clear from the context of his published work that pathologising poverty was not at all what he himself had in mind: the structural origins of child abuse were his own major target (Parton 1985). The problem was that this discourse could be falsely misappropriated by policy-makers with different agendas from Parton's own. In a later publication (N. Parton 1990 pp. 10-13) he also acknowledges that his 1985 analysis failed to fully take into account the (probably much under-reported) occurrence of physical abuse in middle class families and did not really explain why physical abuse only happens in a small percentage of families who are poor.

However, from the point of view of Thatcherite policy-makers, Parton's 1985 analysis could be absorbed, albeit inappropriately, within a particular construction of child abuse. For such policy-makers now socially constructed it as one more product of that residuum of society demonized by Thatcherism as being (allegedly) responsible for most other (alleged) social ills such as: "scrounging", "delinquency", crime, riots, "national disloyalty in time of war" and strikes.

The family dysfunction analysis of Dale and his colleagues was also comforting for Thatcherism on two counts: first, it diverted attention away from any alternative explanations of child abuse which might hint at structural causes; second, the focus on a supposed minority of dangerous families also diverted attention away from the vast majority of allegedly "decent" families which, in Thatcherite mythology, were the bedrock of British democracy.

In this context, it is now easy to see why Government documents such as "Protecting Children" should eagerly incorporate elements of such discourses. That document prefaces itself by noting the limitations of risk checklists - and then implicitly incorporates the principles of those same checklists using criteria based on individual, family and class pathologies (McBeath and Webb 1990-1).

These, then, were most of the features which shaped welfare policy towards child abuse post-1979: a desire to reduce social work intervention which was both ideologically undesirable and expensive; a shift from treatment and prevention to bureaucratic identification of dangerousness (i.e. investigation) and punishment; ghettoising "dangerousness" in a small, allegedly delinquent, minority of the population within the lower orders of society. It was therefore not surprising that to a large extent child welfare in Britain became largely confined to the investigation of child abuse cases (Saraga 1993, Pringle 1995, Gray et al. 1996 and forthcoming). In effect this was the model of child welfare, so characteristic of Britain by the late 1980s, which is known as Child Protection.

The actual bureaucratic machinery of Child Protection was developing over quite a long period but key developments were the publication by the Government of: the guideline document "Working Together: A Guide to Inter-agency Co-operation for the Protection of Children from Abuse" (HMSO 1988); the Children Act (HMSO 1989) together with nine volumes of guidance issued to supplement it; the revised version of "Working Together" (Department of Health 1991) also issued to coincide with the Children Act; and the "Memorandum of Good Practice" (Home Office 1992) relating to initial child abuse interviews with children.

Indeed, one of the most striking features of Britain's Child Protection model is the mountain of regulations and guidance issued by the central Government to control it and the degree to which the practice of social workers and other professionals is officially scrutinised and regulated (see Cooper et al. 1992 for a comparison in this regard with French practice). This characteristic no doubt partly reflects the high media profile of child abuse in Britain. It may also reflect the fact that, for historical reasons, England and Wales is a far more centralised state politically than most other nations in the European Union, as witnessed by the lack of regional government here. Some would also argue that since Mrs. Thatcher's election centralisation has been advanced, despite the rhetoric of the Government about decentralisation.

Whatever the case, day to day operation of the Child Protection model occurs at a local level. From 1988 policy and practice around Child Protection was to be co-ordinated and monitored in each area of Britain by a local Area Child Protection Committee (ACPC), on which were (and indeed still are) represented at senior managerial level all the major local agencies involved in Child Protection cases including social services, health, education and the police. Each ACPC has issued written instructions to all professionals in its area who may be involved in Child Protection cases as to how those cases should be dealt with procedurally, based upon central Government regulations and guidance. Indeed, the concept of procedure is pivotal to the ethos of Child Protection. There is not space here to detail the full range of procedures relevant to Child Protection cases. Comments on various aspects of those procedures are made later in this chapter. Suffice it to say at this stage that key elements in these procedures are:-

(a) Use of Child Protection Case Conferences (representing local agencies and, usually now, parents) to gather together initial information on alleged cases of child abuse. These are co-ordinated by the professional staff of the local Social Services Department. It makes decisions about "registration" of children (see below) and may also make recommendations about future action, which is ultimately decided by the particular agency which has prime responsibility for each specific action (e.g the police in relation to criminal investigation).

The role of parents in conferences has been the subject of much attention and research, often sponsored by central Government (for instance, and most extensively, Thoburn et al. 1994). The overall outcome of this research has tended to emphasise the advantages of parental participation. However, some voices within practice have been keener to point out problems relating to actual power differentials between parents and professionals, the lack of distinction made between abusing and non-abusing parents (Campbell 1995) and the tensions between partnership with parents and putting the rights of children first (Biss 1995).

(b) The possibility of registration of children on a national child abuse Register compiled locally by Social Services Departments. Registration is a contentious issue and doubts have been raised about it in terms of civil liberties, local variability and its effectiveness or otherwise in assisting the protection of children (Gibbons et al. 1994).

(c) Massive procedural guidance exists on enqiries and assessment relating to child abuse, but much less so in relation to therapeutic help - except in so far as the latter might hinder the former. Following the Cleveland Report in 1988 (see below), there has been considerable governmental concern to separate out "therapeutic" intervention from enquiry and investigation, with the latter seemingly taking precedence over the former. This is most clear in the so-called "Memorandum Of Good Practice" (Home Office 1992).

(d) In line with the above, there has been an increasingly clear development of priorities in Child Protection being skewed towards the criminal aspects of child abuse cases rather than the social welfare ones. Once again, evidence for this exists in the "Memorandum" and also in the lack of Government scrutiny about levels of therapeutic help available compared to their concern about procedural rectitude regarding enquiries and assessment. In addition, the Children Act 1989 was explicit in its intention to make the routes by which children enter the care system fully dependent upon rigorous judicial scrutiny (Allen 1992).

There is one vital feature of the post-1979 British child welfare world which so far I have deliberately left out. Although it has reinforced some of the trends we have already noted, its main effects have been to undermine the Thatcherite analysis, to create unsettling complexities within the otherwise simplistic world of Child Protection, and (just perhaps) to point the way towards a future for the protection of our children which is more effective than anything we have so far experienced in our modern history.

That missing element is the rediscovery of child sexual abuse, and with it, the re-emergence of gender as a central dynamic in violence towards children. The re-emergence of sexual abuse came late compared to physical abuse, emotional abuse or neglect. In Britain it did not begin to reach the mainstream of child welfare professionals until perhaps the mid-late 1980s. Moreover, unlike the case of physical maltreatment, sexual abuse initially came to notice in Britain in the teeth of professional opposition and resistance: though professionals (especially male professionals) were quick to colonise the subject once it had been forced onto the welfare agenda by others (Armstrong 1991 and 1996, Hudson 1992, Pringle 1995).

Where, then, did the impetus for its re-emergence originate if not from within the "helping" professions? The answer is clear and alerts us to the essentially subversive potential of sexual abuse within the welfare establishment. For sexual abuse was initially pushed onto the welfare agenda in the U.S. and the U.K. by people who had been sexually abused and by their allies. The majority of those people who pushed the issue forward were female (Rush 1974 and 1980, Armstrong 1996, Finkelhor 1979 and 1984, Dominelli 1986, Davis et al. 1987, Nelson 1987, Kelly 1988, Kidd and Pringle 1988, McLeod and Saraga 1988). What also united most of these people was that they explicitly viewed child sexual abuse using a feminist or pro-feminist lens. For them child sexual abuse was predominantly an issue of gender politics.

It seems unlikely that child sexual abuse would have become such a major issue in the U.S. or the U.K. without the advocacy of strong, highly politicised feminist movements throughout the 1970s, 1980s and 1990s - in particular radical feminist movements. In considering why sexual abuse has not achieved the same prominence elsewhere in Europe, even in those countries alert to other forms of child abuse, this factor has to be a central consideration (Pringle 1993 and 1996).

Debate continues in Britain, as elsewhere, about whether the prominence accorded to child sexual abuse is justified. On the one hand, it can be argued that the attention now devoted to sexual abuse has to some extent resulted in too little attention being paid to other forms of child maltreratment, in particular neglect and emotional abuse. On the other hand, while controversy still exists about precise prevalence levels of sexual abuse in the United Kingdom (Pringle 1995 p.46), few commentators in this country would now dispute the fact that it is a widespread and major social problem.

Speaking personally, I am quite prepared to accept the upper estimates of its prevalence in our society using relatively wide definitions of what constitutes sexual abuse: perhaps 1 in 5 (Finkelhor et al. 1990) or 1 in 3 (Kelly et al. 1991) of the population under the age of 18 years. Moreover, if the discovery of the sexual abuse problem has diverted attention from other forms of abuse, then one can argue that is a reflection of reprehensible social and professional attitudes and not an argument for paying less attention to sexual abuse. Our society and its welfare professionals should be able to face the enormity of sexual abuse and pay due attention to other forms of abuse which also present major social challenges. Anyway, it is often impossible to separate some forms of abuse from one another: for instance, sexual abuse surely entails emotional abuse too.

Such massive estimates of child sexual abuse in themselves partly indicate why in the past there had been a resistance to placing the issue back on the child welfare agenda; why it took around seventy years for its rediscovery. For the causation necessary to explain such high levels of abuse cannot be based on the idea of a tiny minority of deviant individuals operating in society. On the contrary, some form of social malaise is more than hinted at in order to explain the prevalence of sexual abuse.

However, the resistance to recognition of sexual abuse may well have more profound origins than simply its prevalence levels. After all, physical and emotional abuse are also recognised as not being uncommon, yet neither was buried so deeply or for so long. Why? What was so special about child sexual abuse?

If we seek a characteristic of child sexual abuse which distinguishes it from other forms of abuse, then one stands out clearly. That characteristic is the gender imbalance among abusers. Most estimates suggest that perpetrators of emotional abuse and neglect are evenly split in gender terms, with perhaps some preponderance of women. As we shall see later, the gender balance in terms of those who commit physical abuse is more debatable but it seems women probably constitute a large minority of such perpetrators (C. Parton 1990 p.43). In contrast to these findings, virtually all the largest and most sophisticated research studies in the U.S. and U.K. concerning child sexual abuse over the last ten years have produced more or less the same result: men or boys constitute about 90% of sexual abusers

(Finkelhor et al. 1990, Kelly et al. 1991). Such statistics have been challenged by certain commentators and there is no doubt that some women do commit child sexual abuse (Hanks and Saradjian 1991, Elliott 1993). The fact remains that the alleged deluge of undiscovered female abusers whom some commentators have predicted will emerge, has signally failed to do so. As far as our (now extensive) evidence suggests, women constitute a small minority of sexual abuse perpetrators: perhaps ten per cent.

Many commentators writing from feminist and pro-feminist perspectives suggest that the social implications which flow from such a gendered analysis of sexual abuse are central reasons why public and professional acceptance of that form of abuse has been with-held for so long (Nelson 1987, Kelly 1988, Kidd and Pringle 1988, MacLeod and Saraga 1988 and 1991, Hearn 1990, Pringle 1995, Armstrong 1996). These commentators point out that the prevalence levels of sexual abuse and the strongly gendered identity of abusers are only explicable if the social construction of masculinity is recognised as a central (though not necessarily exclusive) factor in those complex processes by which sexual violence against children is generated (see Pringle 1995 pp.170-180 for a detailed analysis of those processes).

It is significant that once child sexual abuse did begin to emerge on mainstream British child welfare agendas in the mid-late 1980s, most welfare professionals tried very hard to ignore a gendered analysis. At first child sexual abuse was firmly incorporated within the new family therapy orthodoxy developing at that time within the welfare professions (Porter 1984, Bentovim et al. 1988).
That perspective remained dominant among welfare academics and professionals until perhaps the early 1990s: in fact, it probably still remains dominant now in the practice of those many professionals who were trained during the 1980s (Pringle 1996).

However, a sustained critique maintained by feminist and pro-feminist commentators has effectively undermined the family therapy position to the point where even some of the its most prominent advocates have publically recognised its inadequacy (Will 1989).

There is not space here to fully outline the weaknesses of the family therapy approach. However, to summarise, we can say that it failed to explain the persistent gender imbalance among perpetrators. It was also fatally weakened when U.S. and U.K. research based on general prevalence studies, unlike clinic samples of abusers (La Fontaine 1990), began to reveal that the majority of sexual abuse did not even occur within the heart of the "nuclear family". It is now clear that most sexual abusers are known to the children they abuse but that abusers tend to be largely peripheral family members, friends, neighbours or significant figures within the community or care milieu of children. With regard to this last point, abusers are sometimes welfare professionals who have contact with children such as nursery nurses, teachers, social workers, foster carers, youth leaders, care workers (Finkelhor 1988, Kelly et al 1991, Pringle 1992, Pringle 1995). The marked presence of men among perpetrators who are welfare workers is maintained, particularly when the relatively small numbers of males working in those professions is taken into account.

Elsewhere (Pringle 1993 and 1996), I have discussed why a gendered analysis of sexual abuse has gained more credibility in Britain than elsewhere in Europe: once again, part of the explanation lies in the persistence of a strong feminist and pro-feminist movement in Britain. Another feature of the British picture which is far less prominent in most other European countries is the awareness within the United Kingdom about the role of welfare professionals as sexual abusers.

Once sexual abuse became accepted by most welfare workers as an important social issue in the late 1980s, reports of children being abused in a variety of care settings grew rapidly. By 1992 the British Government itself was sufficiently alarmed to set up an inquiry into how staff in welfare settings could be recruited and trained so as to reduce the problem (HMSO 1992). Some commentators heavily critiqued the effectiveness of that enquiry report (the Warner Report) because of its total lack of any gendered analysis of sexual abuse (Pringle 1992, 1995).

The spate of public scandals about abuse by welfare workers has continued unabated since 1992: in fact, if anything they have increased. The result is that in June 1996 the Government announced a national Children's Safeguards Review (Community Care 1996). There is no longer a debate in Britain about whether sexual abuse committed in welfare settings is a major problem: more or less everyone now accepts that it is. The debate in Britain is about how to stop it. Perhaps the new Safeguards Review will at last include a gendered analysis of sexual abuse in its considerations. This commentator at least hopes so: otherwise the review will be as ineffective as all its predecessors.

It is important to note that although it was clearly the recognition of sexual abuse as a general social issue which then led to an awareness of the problem in welfare settings, that raised awareness extended to physical and emotional, as well as sexual, abuse committed in schools, childrens' homes, nurseries etc..

There is another important example in Britain of issues arising out of sexual abuse promoting debates about other forms of abuse. For along with the developing acknowledgement of gender as a major factor in the generation of sexual abuse, a debate has ensued about the role of gender in understanding the nature of physical abuse too. We noted above that Nigel Parton recognises his earlier social and class-based explanations of physical abuse have flaws (N. Parton 1990): why should such abuse happen in only a small minority of poor families? why do we have a growing awareness that physical abuse also occurs in relatively wealthy families?

Without suggesting that there is any monocausal explanation of physical abuse, some commentators are now arguing that gender should be considered more centrally than hitherto as one important factor among others in explaining the phenomenon of physical abuse. On the one hand, some research (Andrews 1994) indicates that men represent a higher proportion of physical abusers than has hitherto been acknowledged. On the other hand, a number of commentators have emphasised the indirect impact of gender oppression on the generation of physical abuse of children: in particular the stresses placed upon women by their gender relationships which then contribute to the physical assaults they make on their children (C. Parton 1990). Meanwhile some commentators in Britain are also highlighting the strong links which are emerging between men's physical and/or sexual abuse of their female partners and the same men's physical and/or sexual assaults on their children (Mullender and Morley 1994). Once again, such analyses are far more common in the U.S. and the U.K. than in much of the rest of Europe.

In considering the impact of the rediscovery of child sexual abuse in Britain after three-quarters of a century, let us finally discuss the effect it has had on the British Child Protection model which developed under Thatcherism. In considering this effect we need to address the way the issue of child sexual abuse has been socially constructed by both the British Government and the media.

Due to the process of that social construction, the effect on the Child Protection model has in fact been both complex and contradictory. In at least two respects the growing awareness of sexual abuse has actually advanced central principles of Child Protection.

First, it has reinforced the idea that social work intervention in families should be minimised to a dangerous minority. In the second half of the 1980s the succession of public scandals relating to child deaths which I described above intensified. These scandals put pressure on the local and central child care authorities to intervene more strongly and extensively in families. Then in 1987/8 what became known as the Cleveland Affair occurred (Campbell 1988, Parton 1991 chapter 4). There is no space to describe this watershed event in detail here. It centred on the actions of two paediatricians and one senior social work manager in an area of North East England, all of whom were prepared to recognise that sexual abuse of children was not an uncommon occurrence. A national debate occurred involving a full public enquiry, centring on whether these welfare personnel had made unwarranted assessments about the occurence of sexual abuse and whether the proper rights and privacy of parents had thereby been infringed.

Regardless of the actual facts of the case which are still open to much heated debate, the conclusions of the public enquiry and the public discourse propagated largely by the media suggested that social workers and other "caring professionals" sometimes intervened excessively in families. Similar controversies and outcomes have occurred since then in relation to other sexual abuse cases. There clearly was (and is) considerable conflict between the discourse concerning insufficient welfare intervention generated by the scandal of child deaths and the discourse about too much intervention resulting from Cleveland. In many ways the latter discourse sits far more comfortably with the economic and ideological imperatives of Thatcherism.

The practical outcome of this clash of discourses can be seen in the shape of the Children Act 1989 which is the most extensive piece of child care legislation ever created in Britain (HMSO 1989). Hailed by many people at the time of its publication as a major achievement, it now appears to this commentator to be a deeply flawed document, not least because of its clumsy inability to reconcile these conflicting discourses (see Allen 1992 for a reasonably balanced and realistic appraisal of the Act in this respect). Without going into detail on this issue, it appears that the overall effect of the Act is to considerably restrict the freedom of social workers to intervene in cases of child abuse, compared with the legal position pre-1989.

The second way in which increased awareness of sexual abuse has effectively promoted Child Protection principles also centres on the public discourses arising out of the Cleveland Affair. For the dominant discourse created by the media and by the recommendations of the public enquiry emphasised the need to privilege legalistic and judicial asessments of sexual abuse cases over social, medical or therapeutic ones. Such an approach fits well with the tendency of the Child Protection model to focus on investigation and judicial disposal rather than on prevention and treatment strategies. This is most clearly apparent in the important Government document published in 1992, the so-called "Memorandum of Good Practice" (Home Office 1992), already mentioned in passing above. That text provides guidance on how to conduct interviews with children which may be recorded and used in criminal proceedings related to cases of child abuse. The privileging of judicial considerations over therapeutic ones in the Memorandum is explicit and illustrated by the fact that it was primarily published by the Government's Home Office (i.e. the department responsible for law enforcement) and only "in conjunction with the Department of Health" (i.e. the department responsible for health and social work).

Thus the growing awareness of sexual abuse, crucially mediated by the discourses arising from the Cleveland Affair, has promoted principles of Child Protection both in terms of minimising welfare interventions into family privacy and in terms of privileging judicial considerations over therapeutic ones.

However, the impact of sexual abuse has been less helpful to the model of Child Protection in other ways. For instance, the extensive research around sexual abuse in the U.S. and the U.K. has thrown up some results which are deeply uncomfortable for anyone seeking to adopt a Child Protection approach.

We have already noted that an important component of that approach is the desire, and alleged ability, to identify dangerous individuals, families or sections of the population. Sexual abuse, perhaps more than any other form of abuse, is resistant to such an approach since repeated research has confirmed that the psychological profile and social functioning of the majority of sexual abuse perpetrators tends to be more or less "normal" (Pringle 1992, 1995). Indeed, the Warner Report (HMSO 1992) which we mentioned earlier had a heavy investment in locating some predictive profile of potential sexual abusers and, to its evident disappointment, failed to find one. In addition, sexual abuse is even more resistant than physical abuse to causative explanations relying on social factors such as poverty, unemployment and poor housing: once again, repeated research into sexual abuse has failed to locate any causative link with such factors (Finkelhor 1986, Pringle 1992). Finally, we have already seen that family-therapy oriented explanations of sexual abuse have largely been discredited in Britain at an academic level.

One side-effect of this state of affairs is that the higher prominence of sexual abuse has thrown into very clear relief the inadequacies of that other critical Government document which we discussed earlier, "Protecting Children" (Department of Health 1988). Readers will recall that "Protecting Children" was written primarily with cases of physical abuse or neglect in mind and incorporated many assumptions about the pathology of abusers in terms of individual, family and social characteristics. From what we have said about physical abuse above, it should be apparent that an assessment model incorporating such assumptions is deeply problematic.

However, what is even more worrying is that "Protecting Children" has routinely been used as the basis for assessments of sexual abuse cases too. If the assumptions it makes about individual, family and social pathology are problematic in relation to physical abuse, then we have to say that all evidence indicates those assumptions are largely irrelevant to the majority of sexual abuse cases. The gap between sexual abuse research findings and the basis of "Protecting Children" has grown so wide that it cannot be long before its use has to be revised. In the view of this commentator, such a revision should, hopefully, be of benefit to assessments of all forms of child abuse.

Finally, and in the long run perhaps most important, developing awareness of sexual abuse as a social problem has damaged the Child Protection model by striking at the heart of the ideological assumptions which underpin that model. For research on sexual abuse more than any other form of maltreatment clearly demonstrates that child abuse can only really be challenged by achieving major changes in the power relations which structure western societies.

Elsewhere (Pringle 1995 pp177-180) I have suggested that adequate explanations of sexual violence as a whole (including child sexual abuse), and effective measures to halt it, have to address structures of social oppression clustered not only around gender but also around interacting relations of power associated with classism, racism, heterosexism, disablism and ageism. In addition, I suspect a similar analysis can be applied to other forms of violence towards children than sexual abuse. For instance, as we will see below, there is reason to believe that the large degree of societal acceptance of physical punishment towards children in Britain plays a considerable role in the generation of physical abuse in this country. Viewed in these contexts a Child Protection model, based as it is on a very narrow field of action, is bound to be hopelessly ineffective.

The model of Child Protection has dominated child welfare responses to child abuse in Britain until now. However since 1995 it has become clear the British Government intends to challenge that dominance. In the last part of this chapter I want to examine why this massive shift in Government policy is apparently occurring, to see where it may lead and to offer a more positive alternative way forward than the Government seems to have in mind.

The way forward
In view of what I have just said about the narrow field of action envisaged within the Child Protection model, it is both ironic and interesting that the Government's own critique of that model since 1995 centres on the degree to which it believes there has been too much intervention prompted by Child Protection practices.

Following the implementation of the 1989 Children Act the Government commissioned a large number of research studies from researchers largely within the mainstream of social work academia, to look at various child care issues primarily in relation to Child Protection. In 1995 the document "Messages From

Reseach" was published by the Government providing a summary of those research outcomes (Department of Health 1995). The conclusions of "Messages From Research" are similar to the outcomes of earlier research carried out by David Thorpe in Britain and Australia (Thorpe 1994). In both cases the central argument is that the bureaucracies of Child Protection do effectively protect most children who need protection - but they are also drawing into their net large numbers of families who do not require such intervention and who would derive more benefit from supportive services rather than the relatively punitive procedures of Child Protection.

These conclusions have to be viewed in the context of the 1989 Children Act. Besides setting out the legislative basis for Child Protection action, the Children Act also contained provisions for the positive support of a much wider category of "children in need". However, while the former functions were defined as statutory obligations and responsibilities imposed on local authorities, the family support provisions had a more permissive framework and the definition of "children in need" was left open to considerable interpretation by different local authorities. Local authorities in Britain are suffering a chronic lack of resources, a scarcity which many commentators would argue is largely due to central Government policies. Given that situation, it comes as no surprise that a recent evaluation by the Government's own Social Services Inspectorate found local authorities were devoting most resources to their statutory obligations under Child Protection procedures at the expense of family support provisions (Department of Health 1996).

Following the publication of "Messages From Research", the Government is now suggesting to local authorities that they should to some extent shift their emphasis away from a Child Protection model to family support one.

We can only speculate as to the underlying agenda of the Government in making this move. First, in the short run it may partly be a matter of relatively simple economics. Local authorities are under increasingly severe economic pressure from central Government and a very considerable portion of local social services' spending goes on Child Protection activity. A reduction in the latter may make further economic restraint imposed by central Government on local authorities more viable. This is because hard-pressed local authorities do not need to spend money freed by that reduction on their family support responsibilities which are defined, as we have noted, far more flexibly than their Child Protection ones.

However, I suspect the main reason for the central Government shift is more medium-term. In the field of adult care, the Government has been pushing forward a policy of encouraging privatisation of services and shrinkage of local authority responsibilities. It may be that the Government wishes to implememt this policy to the same extent in the field of child care. If so, it would be politically much easier to privatise local authority services devoted to family support than to privatise more politically sensitive Child Protection functions. Some commentators might even argue that the long-term strategy of central Government may be to wholly dismantle local government in Britain. If that was a strategy, then shrinkage now of sensitive and high media-profile Child Protection functions would ease the way.

My own view is that Child Protection as a welfare response to child abuse is inadequate and should be dismantled. However, my reasons for this judgement are very different from those in "Messages From Research" and the services which I would advocate are very different from those apparently envisaged by the Government. Elsewhere (Pringle 1996, Gray et al. 1997) I have outlined my arguments in considerable detail. Here, I will merely summarise them.

I believe Child Protection should be dismantled because it does not work. We are devoting considerable resources to a system of legalistic investigation largely devoid of any prior preventative action or of any treatment services to follow on from investigation. Moreover, contrary to "Messages From Research", I do not believe the legalistic investigations which are undertaken protect most children who are being abused.

Let us take the case of physical abuse first: I will address the evidence relating to sexual abuse afterwards. On the one hand, general prevalence studies in Britain clearly indicate that severe physical chastisement of children is far more common than would be suggested by the numbers of children registered for physical abuse (Hallett 1995). On the other hand, we have to remember that in Britain physical chastisement is not in itself socially condemned: there is no legal injunction against it as there is in many of the Nordic countries (Davies and Sale (1989). In other words, up to a point physical chastisement in Britain is socially constructed as "normal". This is also borne out by statistical evidence. Hallett (1995 p.34) reports a recent British research study indicating that only 9% of children had never been smacked. Moreover, she argues that:

"given the apparently widespread recourse to physical chastisement in British child-rearing practices, the children who are registered for physical abuse may not be readily distinguished in terms of their injuries from others in the same age groups from similar backgrounds" (Hallett 1995 p.39).

There are obviously two ways of looking at this, as Hallett implicitly acknowledges. On the one hand, we could draw on this material to argue from a British perspective, as "Messages From Research" (Department of Health 1995) seems to do, that the Child Protection system suceeds in picking up most really serious cases of physical abuse (i.e. child deaths and serious medical damage) - along with many others which are less worthy of attention in terms of our societal norms. On the other hand, we could adopt a more "Nordic" perspective and regard the facts that (i) perhaps 16% of British children are subjected to severe physical chastisement (Hallett 1995 p.34) and (ii) most of these children never reach the Child Protection system as warranting great concern. My view corresponds to the latter perspective rather than the former.

The failure of the Child Protection system to pick up the majority of instances of child abuse is more clear-cut when we consider the data on sexual abuse. For there is without doubt a massive gap between the huge societal prevalence rates for sexual abuse (e.g. Kelly et al. 1991) and the much smaller rates of children placed on child abuse registers (Hallett 1995 pp.33-37). Our welfare services are simply not detecting the vast majority of child sexual abuse cases which are out there in our society.

Moreover even when the Child Protection system does detect cases of sexual abuse, it often signally fails to achieve any positive result even in its own narrowly defined terms. For instance, recent Government-sponsored research (Davies et al. 1994) has demonstrated that the vast majority of the thousands of interviews taped in accordance with the "Memorandum of Good Practice" (see above) are never even presented to the Government prosecutors who decide whether to take child abuse cases to the legal courts. So, even investigations under the Child Protection procedures often fail to secure the protection of children. The Child Protection model frequently provides neither prevention, protection nor therapeutic help for children.

Turning now to the family support model of services advocated by the Government since 1995, I am equally sceptical about its value in dealing with child abuse for three reasons. First, as I mentioned earlier, I suspect the agenda for this advocacy is largely one of cost-cutting - which does not imply a particularly positive outcome for service users.

Second, family support as a response to child abuse, particularly sexual abuse, may well be a recipe for protection of perpetrators rather than children who have been abused. This judgement is based on a critique I have provided elsewhere (Pringle 1993 and 1996) of the family support-oriented policies which already exist in several other European countries, most notably the Netherlands (de Ruyter 1990 pp. 33-4, Armstrong and Hollows 1991 p.147, Van Montfoort 1993), Belgium (Marneffe et al. 1990 pp.7-10, Armstrong and Hollows 1991 p.148), Germany (Hutz 1990 p.60, Armstrong and Hollows 1991 pp.152-4), Austria (Paulischin 1990 pp.5-6), and France (Cooper et al. 1995). If these continental systems represent a model for a British family support approach, then I am not optimistic about its ability to ensure the safety of children.

Family support may be a more realistic strategy in some cases of "moderate" physical abuse, given that poverty etc may be a contributory factor in a number of cases, but by no means all. However, it is not clear what it offers in very severe cases. Moreover, even where the abuse is "moderate", family support does not seem to address two factors which, as we have seen earlier, also seem to be key in many cases of physical maltreatment in Britain: issues of gender oppression; societal endorsement of physical violence as a means of punishing children

My third reason for scepticism about a family support model of service provision is that, as we have seen earlier in this chapter, Britain did adopt a continental-style family-support based response to child abuse in the period 1945-late 1970s and it was not a success - largely because it failed to protect many children.

So, if I advocate dismantling of the Child Protection system but am also sceptical of the alternative model now promoted by the Government, what is my suggestion for the future? Elsewhere (Pringle 1996, Gray et al. 1997) I have tentatively outlined what I refer to as a community-oriented response to child abuse. This model is designed largely with sexual abuse in mind but may well be applicable to other forms of child abuse too. It is based on a perspective which regards child abuse as primarily the outcome of a complex interaction of oppressive power relations structuring our society in all its aspects, ranging from the intrapsychic domain through to the societal one (see Pringle 1995 p.213 and, for a more general analysis of societal power relations, Adams 1996). In such a context, I argue concerted anti-oppressive action is required within all those domains in order to counter violence to children.

One particularly crucial area for positive action are the local communities in which our children live. Drawing partly upon experiences of "user empowerment" developed largely in relation to the disability movement in Britain (Beresford and Croft 1993), I have suggested that effective preventative, protective and therapeutic services for children and families can be provided to a considerable extent by "ordinary" people living within those communities. However, this would only be viable if their efforts were underpinned by local and central government in terms of finance and enabling support provided by welfare professionals.

Using sexual abuse as a model for this community-oriented approach, we can suggest that as far as energy, commitment, and understanding are concerned the key figures within that approach will be adult survivors, non-abusing parents of child survivors and their allies both in local communities and in welfare professional agencies. British examples for these kinds of local networks already exist both in theory (Pringle 1995 pp204-219,; Smith 1994, 1995; Gray et al. 1997) and in practice (Pringle 1995 pp196-201, Gray et al. 1997).

There are numerous survivor-led and/or survivor-centred community-based groups around Britain carrying out major work in their localities: determining the amount and form of services required; putting pressure on local and/or central government to provide services to match those requirements or, indeed, to provide resources so the local groups can deliver them directly; raising awareness in their communities about the extent of abuse in those communities and the dynamics of sexual abuse; evaluating services already provided; providing invaluable therapeutic support to survivors and non-abusing parents. Elsewhere (Pringle 1995 pp. 196-201) I have described one such project.

Such a community-oriented model is probably applicable to other forms of child abuse as well. In fact, in some ways it may be more applicable given that there is often far less stigma within British local communities attached to individuals who perpetrate emotional abuse or even physical abuse than those who commit sexual abuse.

Certainly the concept of a community-oriented response to child abuse needs to be developed much further than is possible in the preliminary sketch offered here. Even so, as I have indicated, we know that theoretical and extensive practice models already exist on which we can build further. Whatever form it takes, there need to be extensive and effective links forged between the "non-professional" services provided by the community within the community for its children on the one hand, and professional networks in the locality on the other hand. The atmosphere of competition which sometimes exists between the "voluntary" and "professional" sectors of welfare in Britain (partly due to the current Government's passion for dismantling state services) must be abandoned: our children cannot afford it.

Moreover, I need to emphasise once again that provision in the domain of the community represents only one field of action in the struggle against violence to children: as I have already noted, that struggle has to be co-ordinated in a range of domains throughout our society. For instance, at the highest societal level we can provide several examples of how the strugggle against child abuse may be carried forward. Community-oriented groups could engage with the central Government political process to seek changes in policy. The local group I mentioned earlier did just this in attempting to put pressure on their local political process to set up a public enquiry into a large child abuse case at a school nursery. Recently, I also wrote on behalf of the same group to a Government minister I had met suggesting that their activity offered a blue-print for action elsewhere. Another example of a societal initiative in Britain is the Zero Tolerance Trust which campaigns nationally (including use of skilful and bold public advertising) for prevention, provision and protection in relation to those children and adults who are abused by men's violence (Pringle 1995 pp.164-7). Such societal initiatives can, and must, be linked to anti-oppressive action within all other domains, including the most individual: i.e. what you and I as individual human beings do about our own actions to counter the violence which so many children in our society endure.

Conclusion

In this chapter we have surveyed welfare responses to child abuse in Britain from medieval times through to the present and beyond. What is striking is that so many of the great debates of the present have close parallels in the agendas being set as early as the 1880s.

What is also striking is that the development of British responses in the century following the foundation of the NSPCC were extremely ideosyncratic when viewed within a European context, apart from the period 1945-1970. In that particular quarter century an approach to child abuse based on an uncharacteristically British sense of social solidarity was in place. This approach, the post-war treatment paradigm, had closer resemblances with current continental responses to child abuse than the Child Protection model which suceeded it. Now at the end of the 1990s, the Government seems set to return Britain once again to a continental family support approach for economic and political reasons.

The contention of this chapter is that Child Protection has not been a success. However, I have also argued that the more continental-style approach based on family support attempted in 1945-1970 was an equal failure. Finally, I have suggested that the prospects for the safety of children are not positive if we now return to the continental model again. Instead I have advocated a radically different approach: preventative, protective and therapeutic services provided by people within local communities supported by local and central Government, linked to a concerted, anti-oppressive society-wide campaign against violence to children. This has never been seen before in either Britain or continental Europe.
Does this radical proposal represent a real possibility for the future - or will we just end up with more of the same?

References

Adams, R. "Social work and empowerment", Macmillan (2nd. edition), 1996.

Ahmad, B. "Black perspectives in social work", Venture Press, 1990.

Allen, N. "Making Sense Of The Children Act", Longman (2nd, edition), 1992.

Andrews, B. "Family violence in a social context:factors relating to male abuse of children" in Archer J. (ed.) "Male violence", Routledge, 1994.

Archer, J. (ed.) "Male violence", Routledge, 1994.

Armstrong, H. and Hollows, A. "Responses to child abuse in the EC' in Hill, M. (ed.) "Social work and the European Community", Jessica Kingsley Publications, 1991.

Aries, P. "Centuries of childhood", Peregrine, 1985.

Armstrong, L. "Surviving the incest industry" in "Trouble and strife", no.21, 1991.

Armstrong, L. "Rocking the cradle of sexual politics: what happened when women said incest", The Women's Press, 1996.

Bell, Q. "Virginia Woolf: a biography vol. 1", Triad, 1976.

Bentovim, A., Elton A., Hildebrand, J., Tranter, M. and Vizard E. (eds.) "Child sexual abuse within the family and related papers", Wright, 1987.

Beresford, P. and Croft, S. "Citizen involvement", Macmillan, 1993.

Biestek, F.P. "The casework relationship", Allen and Unwin, 1961.

Biss, D. "Invited comment" in "Child abuse review", vol.4 no.3, 1995.

Bowlby, J. "Child care and the growth of love", Penguin, 1953.

Campbell, B. "Unofficial secrets", Virago, 1988.

Campbell, B. "A question of priorities" in "Community care", 24-30 August 1995.

Cannan, C. "Changing families, changing welfare", Macmillan, 1992.

Clarke, J. "The comfort of strangers: social work in context" in Clarke, J. (ed.) "A crisis in care: challenges to social work", Sage, 1993.

Clarke, J. and Langan M. "The British welfare state: foundation and modernization" in Cochrane A. and Clarke, J. (eds.) "Comparing welfare states: Britain in international context", Sage, 1993.

Cochrane, A. "Challenges from the centre" in Clarke, J. (ed.) "A crisis in care: challenges to social work", Sage, 1993.

Cooper, A., Hetherington,R., Baistow,K., Pitts, J., and Spriggs, A. "Positive child protection: a view from abroad", Russell House Publishing, 1995.

Dale, P., Davies, M., Morrison T., and Waters, J. "Dangerous families", Tavistock, 1986.

Davis, E., Kidd, E. and Pringle, K. "Child sexual abuse training programme for foster parents with teenage parents", Barnardos, 1987.

Davies, G., Wilson, C., Mitchell, R. and Milsom, J. "Videotaping children's evidence: an evaluation", HMSO, 1994.

Davies, M. and Sale, A. "Child protection in Europe", NSPCC, 1989.

Department of Health "Protecting children: a guide for social workers undertaking a comprehensive assessment", HMSO, 1988.

Department of Health "Working together - under the Children Act: a guide to inter-agency cooperation for the protection of children from abuse", HMSO, 1991.

Department of Health "Child protection: messages from research", HMSO, 1995.

Department of Health "SSI report on family support services", HMSO, 1996.

de Ruyter, M.H. "The Netherlands" in Davies, M. and Sale, A. (eds.) "Child protection in Europe", NSPCC, 1990.

Dingwall, R. "Some problems about predicting child abuse and neglect" in Stevenson, O. (ed.) "child abuse: public policy and professional practice", Wheatsheaf, 1989.

Dominelli, L. "Father-daughter incest: patriarchy's shameful secret", Critical Social Policy, Summer, 1986.

Elliott, M. (ed.) "Female sexual abuse of children: the ultimate taboo", Longman, 1993.

Fawcett, B., Featherstone, B., Hearn, J. and Toft, C. (eds) "Violence and gender relations: theories and interventions", Sage, 1996.

Ferguson, H. "Rethinking child protection practices: a case for history" in Violence Against Children Study Group "Taking child abuse seriously", Unwin Hyman, 1990.

Ferguson, H. "Cleveland in history: the abused child and child protection, 1880-1914", in Cooter, R. (ed.) "In the name of the child: health and welfare, 1880-1950", Routledge, 1992.

Ferguson, H., Gilligan, R. and Torode, R. (eds.) "Surviving childhood adversity: issues for policy and practice", Social Studies Press, 1993.

Finkelhor, D., L.M. Williams, N.Burns "Nursery crimes: sexual abuse in day care", Sage, 1988.

Finkelhor, D., Hotaling, G., Lewis, I. and Smith, C. "Sexual abuse in a national survey of adult men and women" in "Child abuse and neglect", vol.14, 1990.

Finkelhor, D. "Sexually victimised children", Free Press, 1979.

Finkelhor D. "Child sexual abuse: new theory and research", Free Press, 1984.

Frost, N. and Stein, M. "The politics of child welfare", Harvester Wheatsheaf, 1989.

Gibbons, J., Conroy, S., and Bell, S. "The operation of child protection registers", HMSO, 1994.

Girodet, D. "France" in Davies, M. and Sale, A. (eds.) "Child protection in Europe", NSPCC, 1990.

Gordon, L. "Heroes of their own lives: the politics and history of family violence, Boston 1880-1960", Virago, 1989.

Gray, S., Higgs, M. and Pringle K. "Services for people who have been sexually abused" in Mckie, L. (ed.) "Researching women's health: methods and process", Mark Allen Publishing, 1996.

Gray, S., Higgs, M. and Pringle, K. "A community-oriented response to child sexual abuse: a way forward" in "Child and family social work", Vol 2, 1997.

Hallett, C. "Child abuse; an academic overview" in Kingston, P. and Penhale, B. (eds.) "Family violence and the caring professions", Macmillan, 1995.

Hanks, H. and Saradjian, J. "Women who abuse children sexually: characteristics of sexual abuse of children by women" in "Human systems: the journal of systemic consultation and management", 2, 1991.

Hearn, J. "'Child abuse' and men's violence" in Violence Against Children Study Group "Taking Child Abuse Seriously", Unwin Hyman, 1990.

Hill, M. (ed.) "Social work and the European Community", Jessica Kingsley Publishers, 1991.

HMSO "Working together - under the Children Act: a guide to inter-agency cooperation for the protection of children from abuse", HMSO, 1988.

HMSO "Children Act 1989", HMSO, 1989.

HMSO "Choosing with care: the report of the committee of inquiry into the selection, development, and management of staff in children's homes", HMSO, 1992.

Hollis, F. "Casework: a psychosocial therapy", Random House, 1964.

Home Office (with Department Of Health) "Memorandum Of Good Practice", HMSO, 1992.

Hudson, A. "The child sexual abuse industry and gender relations in social work" in Langan, M. and Day, L. (eds.) "Women, oppression and social work", Routledge, 1992.

Hutz, P. "West Germany" in Davies, M. and Sale, A. (eds.) "Child protection in Europe", NSPCC, 1990.

Kelly, L. "Surviving sexual violence', Polity, 1988.

Kelly, L., Regan, L., and Burton, S. "An exploratory study of the prevalence of sexual abuse in a sample of 16 - 21 year olds", Polytechnic Of North London, 1991.

Kempe, C. H. "The battered child syndrome" in "Journal of the american medical association", vol.181(1), 1962.

Kidd, L. and Pringle, K. "The politics of child sexual abuse" in "Social work today", vol.20(3), 1988.

La Fontaine, J. "Child sexual abuse", Polity Press, 1990."

Langan, M. "New directions in social work" in Clarke, J. (ed.) "A crisis in care: challenges to social work", Sage, 1993.

Lister, P. G. "Child protection work in Scotland: an introduction for social work students in E.U. countries" in Birks, C. (ed.) "Child abuse in Europe", emwe-Verlag-Nurnberg, 1995.

Lorenz, W. "Social work in a changing Europe", Routledge, 1994.

McBeath, G. B. and Webb, S.A. "Child protection language as professional ideology in social work" in "Social work and social services review", no.2, 1990-1.

MacLeod, M. and Saraga, E. "Challenging the orthodoxy: towards a feminist theory and practice" in "Feminist review", no.28, 1988.

MacLeod M. and Saraga, E. "Clearing a path through the undergrowth" in Carter, P., Jeffs, T. and Smith, M.K. (eds.) "Social work and social welfare yearbook 3", Open University Press, 1991.

Marneffe, C., Boemans, E. and Lampo, A. "Belgium" in Davies, M. and Sale, A. "Child protection in Europe", 1990.

Mullender, A. and Morley, R. (eds.) "Children living with domestic violence: putting men's abuse of women on the child care agenda", Whiting and Birch, 1994.

Nelson, S. "Incest: fact or myth", Strathmullion, 1987.

Parton C. "Women, gender oppression and child abuse" in Violence Against Children Study Group "Taking child abuse seriously", Unwin Hyman, 1990.

Parton, C. and Parton, N. "Child protection, the law and dangerousness" in Stevenson, O. (ed.) "Child abuse: public policy and professional practice", Wheatsheaf, 1989.

Parton, N. "The politics of child abuse", Macmillan, 1985.

Parton, N. "Taking child abuse seriously" in Violence Against Study Group "Taking child abuse seriously", Unwin Hyman, 1990.

Parton N. "Governing the family: child care, child protection and the state", Macmillan, 1991.

Paulischin, H. "Austria" in Davies, M. and Sale, A. (eds.) "child protection in Europe", NSPCC, 1990.

Perlman, H. H. "Social casework: a problem-solving process", University of Chicago Press, 1957.

Pollock, L. "Forgotten children", Cambridge, 1983.

Porter, R. (ed.) "Child sexual abuse in the family", Tavistock, 1984.

Pringle, K. "Child sexual abuse perpetrated by welfare personnel and the problem of men" in "Critical social policy", no.36, 1992.

Pringle, K. "Child sexual abuse committed by welfare personnel: British nd European perspectives", paper presented at fourth European conference on child abuse and neglect, University of Padova, 1993.

Pringle, K. "Men, masculinities and social welfare", UCL Press, 1995.

Pringle, K. "Protecting children against sexual abuse: a third way?", paper presented at conference on "Human services in crisis: national and international issues", Fitzwilliam College, University of Cambridge,
September 1996.

Reder, P., Duncan, S. and Gray, M. "Beyond blame: child abuse tragedies revisited", Routledge, 1993.

Rich, P.B. "Race and empire in British politics", Cambridge University Press, 1990.

Rush, F. "The sexual abuse of children: a feminist point of view" in Connell, N. and Wilson, C. (eds.) "Rape: the first sourcebook for women", American Library, 1974.

Rush, F. "The best kept secret: sexual abuse of children", McGraw-Hill, 1980.

Saggar, S. "Race and politics in Britain", Harvester Wheatsheaf, 1992.

Saraga, E. "The abuse of children" in Dallos, R. and McLaughlin, E. (eds.) "Social problems and the family", Sage, 1993.

Smith, G. "Parent, partner, protector: conflicting role demands for mothers of sexually abused children" in Morrison, T., Erooga, M. and Beckett, R.C. (eds.) "Sexual offending against children: assessment and treatment of male abusers", Routledge, 1994.

Smith, G. "The protector's handbook", The Women's
Press, 1995.

Thompson, N. "Anti-discrimimatory practice", Macmillan, 1993.

Thoburn, J., Lewis, A. and Shemmings, D. "Paternalism or partnership? Involving families in the child protection process', HMSO, 1994.

Thorpe, D. "Evaluating child protection', Open University Press, 1994.

Van Montfoort, A. "The protection of children in the Netherlands: between justice and welfare" in Ferguson, H. Gilligan, R. and Torode, R. (eds), "Surviving childhood adversity", Social Studies press, 1993.

Will, D. "Feminism, child sexual abuse, and the (long overdue) demise of systems mysticism" in "Context", no.9, 1989.

Williams, F. "Social policy: a critical introduction", Polity, 1989.

Child Protection in Finland

By Riitta Tuomisto and Elina Vuori-Karvia

History and legislation

Introduction

Finnish society is in a situation of major change today. Until the 1990's people were used to thinking that the wealth of the whole nation (and at the same time the wealth of a single citizen) would grow year by year. There was lack of labour force in many branches and social policy researchers were discussing the theme of the middle class, which was seen as growing. After the period of the 1970's (when the topic of the discussion was in marxist terms on the role of the labouring class and the existence of class society as a whole) in the 1980's those ideas seemed old fashioned, because "the new society" appeared to promise so much good to everyone now and for ever. Social work and child protection were marginal themes. The welfare state had organized the services and benefits for families so well that most of the need for daycare was satisfied; there were alternatives for parents who preferred home care etc.

Then came the depression and unemployment grew suddenly from 5-7 percent to near 20 percent of the labour force. There was a bank crisis at the same time. The state had to come to save the situation with about 70 thousand million Finnish Marks. Politicians informed the people that they had consumed too much and that was why the whole nation was now in this situation.
Before the depression there had been an enormous growth in the rates for bankloans. For those who had bought an apartment at the wrong time it was destructive especially if at the same time they were left without work. In the first years of the 1990's a common discussion was the division of the people into A and B-citizens and moreover into C-citizens. Many saw membership of the European Union (EU) as solving this new situation. Before Finland became a member of the EU there were almost the same number of people who regarded the EU as a threat to Finland. In 1996 unemployment is neither growing any more nor declining essentially.

Sipilä (1989) in his book on social work divides the development of the welfare state into three periods. During the first period the development of the social policy achievements was linked with industrialization. Social policy was social policy for wage-earners. The task for social work was to arrange the maintenance of the people, who could not obtain it by work. In the second phase social policy and social services reached the whole population. For social work there was the further task of arranging the maintenance of those people who for some reason or other are outside "the working society". Socialization takes the place of open control and a checking system. In the third phase the development of the welfare state is ended. There is the crisis, and the criticism of the welfare state, which may lead to cutting down social allowances and services, removal of the form of action of the welfare state or destruction of the whole idea of the social welfare state (Sipilä 1989,-78-91).

What are the goals of social work in this situation? When the ideological, economic and political atmosphere has changed drastically, what are the changes in practice in social work? Is it only to "let it be" or receive what "is given"? What are the new opportunities? Do the actors within social policy and social work have the ability to reflect their goals, position, tasks and practice in the new situation? Can they act as quickly as the cutting axe of the government? A child cannot wait, she needs care and safety today and tomorrow.

About the history of abuse and neglect

The history of Finnish child protection is often written as part of the history of the welfare state and social policy achievements (Jaakkola 1991, Vähätalo 1994). This history is seen as a picture where orphans and beggars marched into the institutions, where they were served food, soap, water and education with moral and religious exhortations. It is a history where the welfare state is the subject. It was a good spirit in which everybody (almost) believed. The question about good child protection was a question about the capacity and strength of the welfare state. This was until 1990's.

Finnish history of child protection is connected with the changes from agrarian culture to welfare state and service culture

The time of agrarian culture, patriarchalism and church: about 1600-1850
The 16th century can be called the time of the responsibility of the owner of the house, if we are searching for some essential point in the system of social responsibility and care. In Finland the basic unit of social security was the household. It was the building in itself, not the family. The responsibility to take care of everyone in the house was settled on the peasant proprietor, because he was the owner of the house (Jaakkola 1991,10). Until 1809 Finland was a part of Sweden. From the 17th century the Crown passed Acts which tried to give the responsibility more to the parish and to the village.

In the middle of the 17th century there was the Great Distribution of the lands. That began the process, where the villages were decentralized and the connections between the members of the household changed, too. The houseowner, who had taken care of his own relatives (and in the same way the others who lived in the house) became gradually the employer. The nuclear family began to separate from the other members of the household (Jaakkola 1991,12-15).
The houses formed a group and in each group there were some poor who walked from house to house. The children, who were orphans or without care of some adult person, were often sold by auction. These auctions were common from the 1830's (Karisto-Takala-Haapo-ja 1991,126-129).
There are stories told by children, who had this cruel fate, which strengthen our information on all kinds of abuse, physical and sexual in some cases(Eenilä 1991).

In the 1830's there started the first philanthropic associations organized by Society Ladies. The objects of their activity were the children.

The infanticides in 1700-1800 centuries
Especially in towns it was not rare for children to be born out of wedlock. In 1841-65 the percentage was about 15, in some towns over 20 percent. It depended partly on the social class of the woman whether it was a stigma to have a child out of wedlock. What were the reasons for infanticides? Shame, cruelty and carelessness, unwillingness and inability to take care of a child?

In spinning houses the biggest group of these women were vagrants and the next largest group were infanticides and abortionists. With the women in the spinning houses lived children.

In late 18th century there were discussions about foundling hospitals. Experience abroad showed that those hospitals failed to take care of children: they did not reduce the mortality rates of children (Pulma-Turpeinen 1987,48-53).
Pulma writes: "In the years 1816-65 in Finland 170 000 children were born out of wedlock, but only 356 infanticides could be proven. In reality, the number was bigger including in addition abortions, but on the whole the problem was quite small" (Pulma-Turpeinen 1987,52 freely in English by RT).

As we know, there has been a lot of child mortality which cannot be proven as infanticide, but there is good reason to believe there are cases which did not come to light. The words of the latter researcher reflect the tendency in social policy research to look for statistics, big numbers, the picture as a whole. In any case the number of 356 infanticides can be regarded as a very large amount. If it happened today we would be shocked. We do not think about the matter much when we COMPARE it with the number of 170 000. But we would feel, think and be shocked by it if we could see these 356 bodies, if they became individuals to us.

The responsibility of organizing social security was placed on the commune, church and finally on the state.
The first important act, which organized more fully the practice in the whole country, was passed in 1852. The act gave general regulations and what should be done in each commune for poor relief. The commune should also organize an executive committee for poor relief. The spirit of the law in 1879 was: "Who is not working, is neither allowed to eat". It was not any more possible to go from house to house begging. The poor houses were established in the biggest cities (which were not very big) (Takala-Karisto-Haapoja.1991,130-136).

"The Association of the Education for Unprotected Children" was founded in 1870. In the beginning of the 20th century the association had nine institutions for children. There were correctional institutions for the boys and other institutions for "unprotected" girls. It was typical for the time, that the association was active from 1870 to 1904, when the institutions became national (Piirainen, Veikko 1974,42).

Finland at the end of the 19th century.
Finland was until late an agrarian country. In 1875 92.3 % of the people belonged to the agrarian population. The other important fact is that Finland was an autonomous part of Russia until 1917. There was not feudalism as in Russia, but instead the problem called "agrarian surplus population". That is to say, there were landowners and tenant farmers. There were also those people who did not have land at all. Because there was not yet enough industry, this population was seen as "surplus-population" (Haatanen 1981,135-140).

The population as a whole increased very slowly until 1750, when it was 420 000. The population was not over one million until the 1810's. From 1815 to 1875 the population grew by 800 000 people.
It was certainly a time of abuse and neglect in many cases. There was not enough food, there was hard work, physical violence, illnesses without medical care, lack of hygiene etc. After the years of famine the first societies for child protection were founded and the institutions were initiated. There were earlier poor houses, which were founded by church and philanthropy and some institutions for children. The legislation relieved the "surplus population" from the chains of forced domicile. People were permitted to settle down where they wanted. The industrialization process was slowly going forward in the towns and there came into being new work places. The first big migration began from countryside to the cities (Haatanen 1981,134140). There were not enough jobs for everyone either.

Prostitution increases during the depressions.
Antti Häkkinen has studied the history of prostitution in Finland. In the years of famine in 1867-68 there was an increase in the number of girls who became prostitutes. The social background of those women was not of the lowest. The most common profession of their fathers was in the field of handicrafts, commerce and skilled workers. An increase in the number of prostitutes is regularly found during depressions. In Helsinki there was about one prostitute per 100 inhabitants in the 1880's. That was about the same proportion as in other large European cities (Häkkinen 1994,101,119).

There has been prostitution during "the good years" of the welfare state, but it was hidden until the 1990's. During the depression in the 1990's street prostitution has become noticed by everyone. The subject has been in the media often in recent years.

There is no exact information about how much prostitution is linked today with child protection. How many of the prostitutes are underaged? How many prostitutes have a child? What are the living conditions of those children?

Child protection 1900-1937
The first high official in the field of child protection was Adolf von Bonsdorff. His task was in 1908 to inspect the reformatory schools and the protective institutions (Piirainen 1974,23).
It says much about the ideological changes in child protection, that in 1890 this inspection of the reformatory schools was made by the Prison Department, from 1918 by the National Board of Education and from 1924 by the Ministry of Social Affairs (Siltanen 1991,51).
Statistics for 1902 show that in Finland there was in that year "2506 poorly cared and illmannered children, of which illmannered were 1041" (Siltanen 1991,53).

The civil war divided the people in two parts in 1917-18. After the war and the independence of Finland there remained a great divide and bitterness between the "reds" and the "whites". The reds talked about rebellion and civil war, the whites about the war of independence. About 20 000 children lost their provider in the war. Almost 90 percent of these children were "the red orphans" (Piirainen 1974,61). The benefits for the whites and the reds were different. The reds got only the minimum for the child, the whites got a pension for the widow and for the child(Piirainen 1974,70). This gap between sections of the population did not become smaller until the years of the Second World War.

In the 1920's many institutions were established. One of the most important organizations "General Mannerheims Child Welfare Organization" was founded in 1920. Two years later was started the Association "Homes for Homeless Children".

In the years of the 1930's the atmosphere was narrow-minded. That can be seen in the discussions regarding the law on sterilization. In the words of the committee report in 1934:" The need for racial purity and public (social) reasons demand

necessarily that the birth of deficient persons, who burden the state and healthy citizens, should be avoided" (Piiroinen 1974,144, freely in English by RT).
The First Child Welfare Act was passed in 1937 after thirty years of preparations and committee working.

Conclusion about the history

If we look at the past in the context of political, cultural, social, economic, ideological and religious circumstances the following factors are especially important:

As regards political history it is important to note that Finland was first a part of Sweden until 1809 and then an autonomous part of Russia in 1809-1917. The other fact of significance was the civil war in 1918, which has had a long-term impact on the political, cultural and ideological atmosphere in Finland.

The myth of consensus in the years of the Winter War (1939-40) and the Continuation War against Russia has now been taken out of "the collective unconsciousness" again by politicians in the current period of depression and mass unemployment. Ideological phrases like "we have got over things together then, we shall do it now again" remind people about this common experience, which "united the people in Finland". This was seen in the voluntary and neighbourly help which was organized by The National Care Organisation during the war.

In addition Sweden gave a neighbour's help to Finland. About 70 000 children were given a temporary home in Sweden during the war (Satka 1994, 299).
Some of the children stayed in Sweden after the war. The number of children is estimated between 6000-15000. Finnish researchers regard the latter amount as being nearer the mark (Pulma 1987,209). In recent years there have been new debates about the children and their experiences. In the years of the war it seemed to be the most important task to save the children's lives. But how did they feel, when they had to leave and their family was staying? And how did they feel, when they returned home, perhaps with quite different conditions to those which they were used to?

After the 1990's we can see a clear change again in the collective consciousness of the people. The first signs of it are seen in a new interpretation of history. In social policy it is seen in the new books written within that perspective which attributes more importance to voluntary work, emphasising communal work instead of the institutions and services organized by the welfare state.

Religion had a significance especially when we consider its importance in shaping attitudes towards unmarried mothers. Up to the beginning of the 19th century some female representatives of the parliament suggested the foundation of shelters for unmarried mothers. In relation to this initiative these representatives pointed out the responsibility of men and the whole society. They pointed out that women were not only (or at all) "guilty", and especially the child was not responsible for the circumstances which existed before her birth (Heinänen 1992, 11-15).

The attitude against unmarried women and their children has changed through history. Finland is nowadays quite secularized and the influence of the church has strongly declined. Religious regulations have lost their significance. This has not happened all over the country: especially in the northern parts of Finland the religious sects regulate very strongly the lives of their members.

The 1960's is the decade which changed considerably the lives of Finnish women and children. Women went to work outside home. The participation in working life is high, as in Scandinavian countries as a whole. In Finland women are working more in full time jobs like Swedish, Danish or Norwegian women. Most Finnish women regard it as natural to support themselves nowadays. The majority of the university students are women nowadays.

After 1960 the essential issue was to organize daycare for the children. After the 1973 Day Care Act the welfare state had to organize daycare services and services for old people because women were not taking care of them as before. For these reasons, it has been said that the welfare state in Finland can therefore be seen as a particular ally for women. It has served their needs in the situation where they try to combine work and family and get equality as a citizen and participant in society (Julkunen 1992).

Within the ideological debate many have emphasized the good outcomes for children which this equality will produce. Others see institutional care as a threat to the child and mother-child relation.

The legislation in child protection in Finland

The title of a book written by Anja-Riitta Siltanen (1991) reflects the development of child protection: "From punishment to rehabilitation, from isolation to family therapy". This is seen also in legislation.

The first Child Welfare Act in 1937

In the first Child Welfare Act the spirit of the law focused on discovering poor conditions, "bad" parents and dividing children very much as before between those who deserved help and care and those who needed discipline and punishment. In the early history of reformatory schools the main principal was in the words of Siltala, to provide education in which work in agrarian culture, christian ethics, and order and punishment were essential (Siltala 1991,102).

Child protection was seen to mean almost the same as a child being taken into care by social officials. The spirit of the law emphasised symptoms, punishment and did not oblige action on after-care.

The need for child protection was justified by the following reasons:
death of parents, physical defect, parents inability to take care of the children, child abuse, negligence towards school attendance or the criminality of the child or young person. Possible actions sanctioned by the law were: counselling, assessment by a probation supervisor or placement in substitute care in an institution or private care. The differences between this and the 1983 Act is remarkable.

The Essential Principles of the Child Welfare Act passed in 1983

The structure of child protection

The first new essential principle was the structure of child protection. The most important function of this protective work was devoted to the task of developing the living conditions of all children. The second task was to organize common services for families with children. These services were to be developed so that the needs of families could be answered. These two themes underline the significance of social development generally within the whole society, and the significance of the question: how far are the needs of children taken into account when communal decisions in housing, health, environment etc. are made.

The main task of child protection was to develop a society where the welfare of all children should be taken into account. That meant more participation and power to influence issues which were earlier regarded as "social" or "child protection" matters.
Following on from these tasks came measures of support by noninstitutional child protection. The means for achieving this was social work and special services which were "tailor-made" for the customer. The social worker is obliged to take the child into care by the law if:
- the living conditions of a child, or the actions of the latter seriously damage the child,
-and by the help of social work, special services or other assistance the situation could not be improved
-and it is to the advantage of the child to take her/him into care.
All of these conditions had to be satisfied: the child had to be in serious danger, the services and other means could not help the family and the child, and taking the child into care really had to be seen as to the advantage of the child in the situation.

There has been much written in recent years about the interpretation of "the advantage of the child", both in the media and in research.
The following themes have often appeared in the media:
-how can social workers have so much power over the families in the interpretation of "the advantage of the child" ?
-because social workers work behind confidentality their faults can never be proved
-social workers take children into care who do not need it.

At the same time a common opinion within children's institutions is that social workers can not practice "real social work" enough (because of bureaucracy and the great number of clients) and/or they do not help families (especially the child) early enough; the children are left in destructive conditions for too long.

Researchers have pointed out the importance of professional skills in child protection and especially in the investigation of sexual abuse (Taskinen,1994), also the difficulty of taking into account and being conscious of different kinds of interpretation. Each of the participants within the situation have thoughts and opinions which are connected with her or his experiences.

General principles

The Child Welfare Act first and foremost emphasizes primary prevention and non-institutional social care. Many social work professionals agree that the law is a good law and it gives the opportunity for child protection to operate more effectively in the areas which should prevent the need for heavy interventions. The problem is not usually the legislation in itself. Instead the question is: how to put it into practice?

The general principles which should guide practice are: the principles of normality, free choice and client centredness. Critics regarding the improvement of services have pointed out that services have been directed to clients who are motivated to get services. To improve services from the client's point of view means the following questions have to be answered: 1) what are the needs of a client as she/he sees them? 2) what kind of help does a client think she/he needs? 3) what kind of services does the client expect to get?

The Child Welfare Act has been said to be more for the protection of the family than the child. Therefore it is essential to define who is the client. Is it the family, one of the parents or the child?

The advantage of the child is the most important principle

The main principle is the advantage of the child. The child has got a juridical position as a subject. The law requires decision-makers to take into account the reality of the child. That means the wishes of the child have to be heard, there has to be sufficient knowledge about the living conditions of the child, and in that situation an evaluation of how different interventions may influence the development of the child. Critics point out that children are not heard enough (or at all) in practice; there is not sufficient knowledge or it is only gathered as a justification for decision-making without inner understanding and orientation to support; and, finally, that it is impossible to evaluate the consequences of the different potential interventions.

How the law protects the client's rights?
The main principle is the advantage of the child. But the law also protects the legal rights of the parents or the provider. The following factors protect either the rights of the parents or the child or both.
- the child's opinion must be taken into account, when it is at all possible
- a child at twelve years has a legal right to speak on her/his own behalf
- the social workers must be aware of the living conditions of the child
- possible interventions must be evaluated against possible consequences
- the opinions of the parties involved shall be heard
- the social officials can consult experts who may be of help in the case
- the social workers are obliged to make a client care plan
- in the case of compulsory admission the county administrative court has to approve the decision
- in a case of emergency admission the time to clarify the situation by social workers is limited to 2 weeks
- the right to recieve after-care
- a twelve year old child can demand an appeal in her/his own case
- visiting rights

There has been discussion and debate on the following issues which are seen not to promote realization of "the advantage of the child":
-the legislation protects the right of access to the child for a parent in cases where social workers believe the best interests of the child would be served by not meeting the parent and/or the child definitely does not want to meet the parent. In these cases changes in legislation will soon be enacted.

Whereas in 1980 the focus of community child protection was on foster care and institutional care, in 1986 the focus was on social work and social services. In 1996 the emphasis is on non-institutional work, where organizations, rehabilitation centres, social offices, and voluntary workers co-operate more fully. Networking, co-operation, developing challenges are the words in current debates about child protection. Are the children protected better now and in which areas?

Current child protection practice in Finland

As already noted above, Finnish child welfare and the entire social system have undergone great changes during the past few years. The deep economic recession has posed serious challenges to the welfare services. Unemployment has increased the need for financial support (living allowances) and has taken resources away from child welfare, despite the concerns expressed by the child welfare organisations. At the same time the administration and financial social welfare and health care have been thoroughly reformed. The new state subsidy system (1993) increases considerably the independence and jurisdiction of the local authorities.

The reform has aroused conflicting expectations. On the one hand, the strengthening of local decision-making is a positive development. On the other hand, there is the danger of increasing regional differences in the provision and quality of the services. It is to be feared that children, particularly those who need child welfare measures, will be ignored because their voice is not heard when decisions are made. Local needs and resources may vary considerably.

Research on the prevalence and context of child sexual abuse, as well as developing and improving expert knowledge in investigating and diagnosing child sexual abuse, have been the main forms of work in this area. Prevention of child abuse has been promoted for example by producing material on non-violent and innovative methods for bringing up children. Research on the co-operation of the authorities in cases of child sexual abuse is in progress.

Finland is a fully-fledged civil society, where a large number of non-governmental organisations play an important part in the social welfare system and run a wide range of activities. The non-governmental organisations are independent, but co-operate actively with the authorities. They extend social services by developing and carrying out new projects and by producing innovations. The characteristics of these organisations include flexibility and willingness to try something new. The organisations also lay great emphasis on the development of voluntary work, which is becoming more and more important since public resources are diminishing.

The non-governmental child welfare organisations strive to defend children's rights and provide a wide range of services for children and families. The voluntary and private child and social welfare organisations in Finland have initiated an array of activities that have later been transferred to local authorities, such as maternity and child health clinics, family guidance centres, shelter homes and school health care.

The non-governmental child welfare organisations run a wide range of activities in the field of child welfare and child care. They provide both preventive and remedial child-welfare services. The preventive services include, among others, family counselling, youth employment projects and recreation camps for children and families. Rehabilitation, therapy and other remedial services are provided by residential care institutions and family homes. The integration of young people is supported by various projects in the institutions in order to prevent exclusion from education, training and working life - from society (Kemppainen 1994).

The means available for child welfare have traditionally been divided into three categories in Finland: general services, prevention, and care. General services include health care, education, cultural activities, and influencing the living environment. These are provided to all children and families without exception. General services also include all forms of financial support and social security. Preventive services in open care are family guidance and counselling, lay-helpers, and hobby activities. Care comprises provision of foster care or residential care, and after care.
In practice, the division into different levels is difficult; the borders between prevention and care are especially blurred.

The purpose of open (non-residential) care measures is to support families and solve the problems so that heavier and emergency interventions can be avoided. Open care measures include improving poor housing conditions, supporting the child's hobbies, arranging income support or providing home help and guidance.

Extra-familial care, i.e. remedial care, is needed when open care measures have proved to be inadequate and when the health or the development of the child is seriously endangered. The child may be taken into care either with the consent of the parents or the guardian or, on special grounds, without their consent. The majority of the placements in care are carried out by mutual agreement; however, the number of compulsory (contested) placements is growing. In all placements, the child must be given the opportunity to be heard. The placements are of fixed duration (Utriainen 1989).

The most common reasons for admission into care are the parents´ or the guardians´ abuse of intoxicant, neglect of the child's care and psycho-social problems and difficulties in up-bringing. Mothers' abuse of intoxicants is also a growing problem in Finland. According to statistics about 60% of child protection measures do happen because of mothers´ alcohol or drug abuse (Taskinen 1994).

Child care institutions have been engaged in a real change during the last few years. Many children's homes have been closed down and instead have become private family homes about which there has been quite a lot of discussion in the media. Since the 1984 child welfare legislation there has been a need to emphasise the primacy of open care measures. Then, it has been important to search for a kind of relationship to residential care, so that long-term residential care and its negative effects might diminish.

The municipal cost reduction policies have diminished the possibilities for helping children and young people. At the same time the problems in families of those children and young people taken in to custody have become more serious. Hard times deepen the difficulties and slow down the capacity to find out solutions. This might lengthen the time of care, which means that the amount of children in custody is growing in spite of the decrease of new custody cases (Muuri 1994).

In 1995 there were 6478 children in custody, which was 75 children more than a year before. In 1995 1592 new custodies were made, which is 132 less than a year before. Ten years before there were about 2000 children more and twenty years ago about 3500 children more in custody than in 1995. Altogether the number of children in extrafamilial care has diminished while custodies have diminished. At the same time as the placements have diminished, the generality of residential care has switched places with family care and other forms of care. While in 1975 there was 51% in residential care, the comparable number in 1995 was 36%. Family care remained the same and placements elsewhere than in family or residential care accounted for 15% of children in 1995.

During the past decade the number of children provided with child care packages has slightly decreased. Today the number is over 18 000 or approximately 1.6% of children under 18. Children provided with open care measures account for about 60% of all children in care. The principal child welfare measures are more and more interlocked, that is, children are provided with open care measures and extrafamilial care. Finland is still an exception in Nordic countries, because nearly 40% of children in extrafamilial care are in institutions; in Denmark and Norway the figure is less than a fourth and in Sweden only a fifth. There is no reason why Finnish children need more institutional care (Muuri 1994). It seems to be a question of different habits in different countries. Even now most of the Finnish children are taken into institutions. Three out of ten children are taken into family care, in other Nordic countries six out of ten. So there is a good reason to ask why any institution is always better than familial care?

Traditional, individual-oriented forms of care have been criticised for being expert dominated, time-consuming and apparently ineffective. These traditional forms of care have been widely replaced by approaches based on systems theory. Also, the new child welfare legislation lays greater emphasis on the children's families, that is, on their natural environment and resources, and it obliges child welfare workers to co-operate with the families.

The Child Welfare Act, which came into force in 1984, identified the supporting of families in the upbringing of their children as the most important principle of child welfare, thus directing the authorities of the Social Welfare office to a concern for the whole family. In family-oriented and individual child welfare the aim is to secure the best interests of children primarily by open care measures, i.e. interventions not involving residence or fostering. This means helping parents or other custodians to understand the child's physical, psychological and social needs.

The child welfare legislation reforms of 1990 emphasise preventive, non-stigmatising, and supportive measures and services. One of the central objectives of the reform was to shift the emphasis of child welfare from extrafamilial care to measures that encourage and support the maintenance of children in their own home.

As a result, work methods of all welfare services, were adapted toward strengthening child rearing by carers. Maternity and child health clinics have expanded and diversified family training, and intensified co-operation with families. In day care, various forms of co-operation supporting parental participation were developed. Also home help services have been developed to support child rearing by parents.

Co-operation between school and home has been increased and diversified, especially at the lower stage of the comprehensive school. In 1990, the services of school welfare officers and school psychologists were fixed by law to make it possible to provide help for problems at an early stage. In 1991 these services were provided in 36% of the municipalities and they cover 45% of the pupils (Kemppainen 1994).

Child Abuse In Finland

Regardless of the fact that Finland was among the first countries to prohibit by law corporal punishment of children (the Child Custody and Right of Access Act of 1983), discussion about child abuse grew very slowly. In other western countries there was a lot of discussion about the issue already at the end of the 1960s and especially in the 1970s. In Finland it was generally felt at that time that the problem did not exist in our society. However some single research studies (Tuovinen 1972, Virkkunen 1974 and 1975) were published, but they got very little attention. In the late 1970s research on the prevalence of sexual abuse increased greatly and continued to grow in the 1980s. Sexual abuse of children had been considered a marginal problem, but as a result of research it is now considered to be one of the gravest threats to the welfare of children in Finland as well (Antikainen 1994).

At the beginning of the 1980s our country's media reported some single cases of incest. The Central Union of Child Welfare in Finland published a wide piece of research about child abuse cases which had become known to officials 1983-1984. Research came to the conclusion that child sexual abuse in Finland was quite a rare phenomenon. Professional journals published some general articles about the subject (Repo 1985). The media and the wider public also began to be interested in child sexual abuse. According to research made in 1985 about 80% of Finnish people had received information about sexual abuse through the media (Peltoniemi 1988).

At the beginning of the 1990s focus of discussion has clearly moved from the features of sexual abuse to those practical problems which workers have to deal with in these cases. The most discussed questions have been around workers´ role and tasks, trust in the methods used for investigations and the co-operation between different parties. From the juridical point of view these questions have been written about, for instance by Räty (1991) and Gottberg et al. (1992); and from the care point of view by Venhola (1991), Varilo and Linna (1992) and Taskinen (1992). The Central Union for Child Welfare in Finland published at the end of 1992 a broadly-based book named "How to help a child" (Antikainen 1994) about investigation and care of physically and sexually abused children.

After Heikki Sariola´s (1990) internationally well known research about child sexual and maltreatment experiences was published, the seriousness of child sexual abuse started also to be disclosed in Finland. According to Sariola´s research 7% of girls and 3% of boys in their fifteens had been treated as an object of sexual abuse. Children's sexual experiences were clearly growing when a child was entering puberty. Only 11% of those having abuse experiences had been abused under twelve years old. Under 14 years old 62% had experienced abuse. According to this research the most critical age seemed to be at the age between 13 and 16 while according to American research the most critical ages seemed to be between 8 and 12 (Finkelhor 1987) and according to Swedish researches the age of abused children was between 8 and 10 years (Dahlström-Lannes 1990).

The extent of abuse in Finland and Sweden seem to be somewhat lower than in many other countries. In Finland and Sweden there seem to be many factors which, according to Taskinen (1994), can be seen to prevent abuse
• the level of general education
• women's independence and working outside homes
• common culture and relatively high moral tone of media
• sauna culture, which lowers the excitement of nudity
• quite relaxed sexual climate, where it is possible to get factual knowledge of sexual issues and to date openly with the other gender.

In Finland we already have those kinds of channels in social and health care which are still missing in many countries: a whole countrywide network of maternity and child health clinics and family guidance centres; also in schools student care; and a large amount of social and health care organisations. Through these channels it is possible in Finland to do a wide degree of preventive work.
In spite of prohibition against children's corporal punishment through the 1984 legislation and the influence on attitudes, about 45% of Finnish people accept corporal punishment in up-bringing. On the one hand the child's position is

defended now more readily than before. On the other hand violence toward children has increased and become more cruel. Child violence happens because of the social and economic position in all kinds of homes. It is growing along with unemployment, alcohol abuse and psychological immaturity. To diminish the violence we need to be able to influence the reasons behind it.

Violence to children is in Finland more common than generally thought. Corporal punishment is often followed by physical violence. About 70% of children under 14 years of age have experienced minor violence. Nearly one tenth has been an object of serious corporal violence. About one fourth of the victims of violence become disabled permanently if they are not given care. Maltreatment is often encouraged by the lack of outside control. The boundaries of families' privacy are often respected so much that people do not interfere with violence happening in other families (Taskinen 1994).

The future

Because in addition to the economic crisis and high unemployment, a political change has also occured in Finland, it is difficult to assess which of the government's or municipalities' policies are the result of economic cuts and which represent changes happening for other reasons. In Finland there is apparently developing a very strong change in social values, even it is sometimes difficult to notice clearly. The situation is not made easier by at the same time growing European integration and the changes demanded by that.

According to Pösö (1996), in Finnish child protection it is typical to believe in the judgement of social and health care officials and their ability to diminish the problems of child protection through professional means. This Finnish trend is seen in many opinions about the quality of problems in child protection; professional skills require working methods.

The difference is also apparent in that it is difficult to use research about child protection carried out in other countries as a support for research work in Finland. Even when the topic for research is the protection and support of children, those studies outside Finland are dealing with quite different kinds of problems and practices.

The newest child protection legislation is characterised by the principle of the child's interest, similar to the welfare principle in England. Supposedly, the content of the principle is very similar. In Finland there has not been guidance to the court about how they should protect the interest of the child in justice and decision making. The decision maker has to seek criteria for the assessment of the child's needs and educational arrangements in the the educational goals defined within the Child Welfare Act and the Child Custody and Right of Access Act, which are in a very general form. A more important role than the court in making decisions about the child's interest is the professionalism and evaluation of the social worker, who puts the legislation into practice (instead in England the emphasis is on formal social control and the role of court)

Finnish child protection seems very reticent compared to many other countries. Of course the latest page in the history of Finnish child protection has focused on the so-called Niko´s case and the polemics in publicity about whether motherhood is only a privilege of the intelligentsia. However, such single cases are not seen as creating central changes of direction in the policies of child protection as happens with similar kinds of cases elsewhere. There are many causes for this colourless approach due to the different kinds of social climate which pertain in different countries. One reason among others is that in Finland not much has been written about child protection, although in the 1990´s it has started to interest many writers and researchers. Single cases have received little media attention and they do not inspire writers to debate as in some other countries.

In Finland, child welfare has been researched only occasionally, with only a few more extensive academic studies; there are, however, numerous papers on a smaller scale, many of which are concerned with residential institutions. No university has a tradition of child welfare research.

The interaction between research and practice has been quite limited. Research findings are not well known in the field and the academic world has no sufficient knowledge of what is happening in the field. Studies have not been systematically evaluated, nor put to good use.

The most typical studies of child welfare have been related to the effects of substitute care on the later life of persons formerly in care. The most researched area is the later stages of young people placed in institutions or community homes because of maladjustment.

The factors which have positively or negatively affected the development of care have been examined in many ways: for example by comparing the effects of various forms of placements (residential care and foster care) with the success of placement; the timing of placements and their permanence, the significance of the experience of separation in placements; and the quality of interpersonal relationships developed in substitute care. In researching the preparation of the placement, documents and decisions, answers have been sought as to the circumstances which have influenced the length of placement.

Despite the lack of research tradition and the scarcity of interaction between research and practice, it is realistic to expect an improvement in the situation in the future. This is already visible. For instance, in recent years, social work research based on the interaction between theory and practice has been more active; its influence will probably be seen in child welfare as well.

Moreover, child protection has not been without criticism in Finnish research. There has been a strong debate about how secondary are children in Finnish child care (Törrönen 1994; Kähkönen 1993), how family problems are directing the policies of child care (Forsberg et al. 1994) or about how many problems the clients of child care have to live with and how little child protection can affect the situation of clients with many different kinds of problems (Forssen 1993). The research work of Tarja Kivinen (1994) is gaining attention. She has pointed out how strongly becoming a client in child protection depends upon the workers' consideration of events. One explanation about why Tarja Kivinen's research outcomes have not affected discussion regarding the parameters and power of professionals' judgements may be that in Finland we are used to emphasising many aspects of child protection. Variety in child protection means, for example, that the selection processes for the client are plentiful, the policies of child protection are rich in diversity and the reasons for needing child protection are as many as life itself. Width of range has been regarded as typical for professional child protection. However neither research nor practice has been willing to systematise that diversity and breadth of range. At least two conditions should, according to Pösö (1996), be fulfilled before preventive child protection relying on professional assessment might be successful. Those are a high level of professional expertise and a large amount of socially supportive resources.

When we combine this assumption with the actual anxiety about diminishing resources in Finnish child care policies, clear regional differences and the lack of child care research and professional scientific education, these might seem to be reasons for generally criticising Finnish preventive and Scandinavian non-specific child care principles. This has not however happened. For we still believe that we can protect children best from a "long distance" by offering them and their families socially supportive opportunities and by avoiding the clear labelling and specifying of their life situation. It can be only a question of time before the anxieties about neglect and the abuse of children appear on the scene.

In Finland questions about child protection have been dealt with as part of social policy, which to some extent resulted in their generality and distance. At the same time helping children's position has also been included in general social policy. Understanding the problems of child protection work as being general, unspecified and socially undifferentiated can also be exhausting.

Instead of legalisation, Finnish child protection has been characterised by a belief in social work, especially kinds of social work other than those characterised by juridical norms and exactness. For the time being it has not been necessary to ground or protect the professionalism of social work and its role. Now there are however indications that the situation is changing: the jurisdiction of child protection is, at least partly, up in the air.

References:

Antikainen, Jorma:Lasten seksuaalinen hyväksikäyttö:Ammatilliset haasteet ja työorientaatiot. Stakes:Sosiaali-jaterveysalan tutkimus- ja kehittämiskeskus. Tutkimuksia 46. 1994.

Dahlström-Lannes, M.:Mot dessa våra minsta. Sexuella övergrepp mot barn. Förlagshuset Gothia. 1990.

Eenilä, Jukka: Ruotiukkoja ja huutolaisia. Muistikuvia entisajan sosiaalihuollosta. Helsinki. 1991.

Finkelhor, D.: The sexual abuse of children:Current research reviewed. Psychiatric Annals,17. 1987.

Gottberg, E.,Ketonen, A.,Koski M-L.:Insestistä rikosoikeudellisena, perheoikeudellisena ja lastensuojelullisena ongelmana. Lakimies,4. 1992.

Haatanen, Pekka: Köyhyys Suomen maaseudulla. Teoksessa Sosiaalipolitiikka, historiallinen kehitys ja yhteiskunnan muutos. Espoo.1981.

Heinänen, Aira : Lapsen tasa-arvoa tavoittamassa. Ensija turvakotien liiton historiikki 1945-1990. Jyväskylä.1992.

Häkkinen, Antti: Maksettua rakkautta. Prostituutiokulttuuria Helsingissä 1860-luvulta nykypäivään. Teoksessa Huono-osaisuus ja hyvinvointivaltion muutos (toim. Matti Heikkilä ja Kari Vähätalo). Tampere.1994.

Jaakkola, Jouko: Yhteisöavusta vapaaehtoistyöhön. Epävirallinen apu suomalaisen sosiaaliturvan kehityksessä. Teoksessa Valtion varjossa (toim. Aila-Leena-Matthies).Helsinki. 1991.

Julkunen, Raija: Hyvinvointivaltio käännekohdassa. Jyväskylä.1992.

Karisto, Antti-Takala, Pentti-Haapoja, Ilkka: Elintaso,elämäntapa,sosiaalipolitiikka. Juva.1991.

Kemppainen, Martti:Trends in Finnish child welfare,in Gottesman- Meir (ed.):Recent changes and new trends in extrafamilial care: an international perspective. London:Whiting & Birch with FICE. 1994.

Kivinen, Tarja: Valikoituminen lastensuojelun asiakkaaksi.Näkökulmia asiakkuuden määrittymiseen. Tutkimuksia 45. Helsinki:Stakes. 1994.

Kähkönen, Päivi: Vanhemmuuden murtuminen. Lapsen huostaanotto sosiaalitoimen asiakirja-aineiston valossa. Julkaisematon lisensiaatintyö. Psykologian laitos. Jyväskylän yliopisto. 1993.

Lapsen etu ja viidakon laki. Toim. Maritta Törrönen. Helsinki.1994.

Lastensuojelulaki 1984.

Muuri, Anu: Lasten elatus,huolto ja lastensuojelu. Helsinki:Stakes;Tilastotiedote 1996/6. 1995.

Piirainen, Veikko:Vaivaishoidosta sosiaaliturvaan.Hämeenlinna.1974.

Pulma, Panu-Turpeinen, Oiva: Suomen lastensuojelun historia. Kouvola.1987.

Pösö, Tarja: Lastensuojelun kaksi maailmaa:englantilaisen jasuomalaisen järjestelmän vertailua. Janus,2. 1996.

Repo, E.: Insesti ei ole fantasiaa - lasten seksuaalinen hyväksikäyttö. Medisiinari,8. 1985.

Räty, T.: Lapsen seksuaalisen hyväksikäytön tutkiminen sosiaalitoimessa. Sosiaaliturva 21. 1991.

Sariola, Heikki: Lasten väkivalta- ja seksuaalikokemukset. Lastensuojelun Keskusliiton Julkaisu 85, Painopörssi oy,Helsinki. 1990.

Satka, Mirja : Sosiaalinen työ peräänkatsojamiehestä hoivayrittäjäksi.Teoksessa

Jaakkola-Pulma-Satka-Urponen: Armeliaisuus, yhteisöapu, sosiaaliturva. Helsinki. 1994.

Siltanen, Anja-Riitta: Rangaistuksesta kuntoutukseen, eristyksestä perheterapiaan. Sosiaalihalli tuksen julkaisuja 21/1990. Helsinki.1991.

Sipilä, Jorma: Sosiaalityön jäljillä.Helsinki.1989.

Taskinen, Sirpa: Lapsen seksuaalisen riiston selvittäminen ja hoito. Stakes. Oppaita 23. Jyväskylä. 1994.

Tuovinen, M.: On real incest. Dynamic Psychiatry (16) 3. 1972.

Utriainen, Sirpa: Child welfare. Volume LXVIII,2. 1989.

Varilo, E., ja Linna, L.: Insesti ja yhteisö. Duodecim 3 vol. 108. 1992.

Venhola, M.: Lasten seksuaalinen riisto. Kunnallislääkäri 7(2). 1991.

Virkkunen, M.: Incest offences and alcoholism. Medicine, Science & Law,14. 1974.

Virkkunen, M.: Victim-precipitated pedophilia offenses. British Journal of Criminology, 15(2). 1975.

Vähätalo, Kari: Suomalainen huono-osaisuuden tutkimus 1980-ja 1990-luvulla.Teoksessa Huono-osaisuus ja hyvinvointivaltion muutos (toim. Matti Heikkilä ja Kari Vähätalo). Tampere.1994.

Child Protection in Ireland

By Helen Buckley

Introduction

Although child protection work has been officially ongoing in Ireland for over a hundred years, it is only within the past decade that child abuse has achieved a significant position on the social and political agenda in Ireland. This has been by way of the unprecedented publicity given to high-profile cases. Revelations of sexual abuse of young children by their families, by the clergy and by other persons in positions of trust, together with recent disclosures about physical abuse of children in residential care settings have combined to focus critical attention on both the existence of child abuse as a serious problem in Ireland, and on the system which deals with it.

This article seeks to highlight particular aspects of child protection practice and policy in Ireland and make some observations on its current orientation. To begin with, the context in which the current system operates will be described having regard, firstly to the historical development of child protection and welfare services and secondly the 'Kilkenny Incest Case', which represented a landmark in the development of child protection in Ireland and highlighted a number of important issues. I will then move on to describe and comment on various elements of current child protection practice within the context of new legislation, policy and procedures. This chapter will be informed by the available literature on child protection in Ireland, and by findings from recent research studies carried out in this country. Legal changes which have lately taken place will be examined, and the effects of the recent politicisation of child abuse in Ireland on policy and practice will be described.

Historical overview of the development of the child protection system in Ireland

The most comprehensive overview of the development of a child protection system in Ireland is offered by Ferguson (1993,1996), who traces its 'official' beginnings from the establishment of the NSPCC (The National Society for the Prevention of Cruelty to Children, first founded in Britain in 1884) in Ireland in 1889, first in

Dublin, and later in other major cities, to become the ISPCC (Irish Society for the Prevention of Cruelty to Children) in 1956. There was some initial distrust of NSPCC, exemplified in the following quote from their 1889 report, cited by Robins (1980:308) that 'a national apathy and a shrinking from interference with what is a mistaken sense of paternal rights' still existed. This, Robins suggests, stemmed less from 'reluctance to interfere' (p.308) than from Catholic suspicions of the society's aims. Irish Catholics found it difficult to accept the good faith of a London-based body, which included members of the Protestant ascendancy in its supporters. However, the religious impartiality of the society became quickly accepted, and it soon became established as an influential and active movement.

The statutory base for child protection in Ireland was provided initially by the Cruelty to Children Acts of 1889, 1894 and 1904. These were superseded by the Children Act of 1908, which represented the legislative framework until the Child Care Act 1991 began its implementation. Ferguson (1996:9) describes the transformation which occurred in the 'casework ideology of child protection' in the early part of the twentieth century from the punitive to the rehabilitative, whereby the function of official agencies was to enforce parental responsibility rather than remove children from the care of their parents. The majority of early referrals to the NSPCC concerned reports of 'neglect', while physical abuse and sexual assault of children accounted for only a tiny proportion of cases (Ferguson 1996). This statistic has been transformed by the recognition of child sexual abuse as a problem in the eighties, though child neglect is still the most frequently reported child abuse concern (Department of Health 1993).

Social changes in Ireland, particularly the 1937 Constitution's ascription of 'inalienable and imperscriptable rights' to parents had an effect on the development of all policy and practice in relation to state intervention into the family. The family was recognised as the 'primary and fundamental unit group of society' (Article 42 of the Irish Constitution). For many years following the establishment of the Irish Constitution, the Catholic Church exerted strong control over the extent of state involvement into what it considered the private domain of family life. Breen, Hannon, Rottman and Whelan (1990) offer the view that up to the 1960's, a distinctive combination of religious orthodoxy, family based production, and the Catholic Church's unrivalled prestige and legitimacy left the family largely outside the sphere of State intervention. Paradoxically, this embracing of the family as a fundamental unit in society was not matched by a parallel effort to enhance the welfare of children. As O'Connor has observed

> One of the puzzling enigmas of Irish Social Policy is the contrast between, on the one had, the clear endorsement of the family as the pivotal unit in Irish society, and, on the other hand, the reluctance up to very recently to initiate legislative reform to protect the most vulnerable members of that group - children (1992:215).

In the second half of this century a number of concurrent developments began to shape the evolution of a more modern child protection and welfare service. The Health Act 1970 devolved the delivery of health and social services to local authorities known in Ireland as Health Boards, to be administered through their various programmes. The 'Community Care' programme became responsible for the delivery of the 'personal social services', including the social work service. The social work service was originally intended to be 'generic' and was expected to cater for the social needs of the elderly, the disabled and to provide a casework service for families and children. Community work was to be used as a channel through which the development of voluntary effort would be encouraged. (Department of Health 1973). Other reforms in child care services were also happening around the same time. In 1968, the Committee on Reformatory and Industrial School Systems was established by the Minister for Education. Its report, known as the 'Kennedy Report', recommended a wide range of reforms in the provision of residential care, including the recruitment of lay workers in an area that had previously been dominated by religious orders, and the replacement of institution-type buildings with small purpose built units. It also laid emphasis on the need for prevention of family breakdown through the development of services, including social work services, in the community.

In 1974, the Irish Government, recognising the need for reform in child care leglisation, established the Task Force on Child Care Services. According to its terms of reference, the Task Force was expected to make recommendations for improved services for 'deprived children and children at risk', to prepare a new Children's Bill to modernise the law, and to make recommendations on the administrative reform necessary to implement these. The recommendations of the Task Force, which reported in 1981, provided the foundations for the more pro-active reforms contained in the Child Care and Protection Bill 1985.

The evolution of the child protection system in Ireland was heavily influenced by international trends and events as well as by its own unique social framework. In the meantime, the 'rediscovery' of child abuse in the 1960's in Britain and the USA with the work of Kempe and Helfer, and the repercussions in Britain of the first child abuse 'scandals' started to have an influence on awareness of the problem in Ireland. The ISPCC, using its links in Britain, acted as a conduit through which these matters to public as well as professional attention. In 1975, the Department of Health set up a committee to discuss the issue of 'non accidental injury to children'. This heavily medically dominated committee agreed that there was a significant problem of non-accidential injury to children in Ireland, and recommended an examination of the position and the suggestion of procedures for dealing with such cases and ensuring the co-operation of parties dealing with it.

The public awareness of child abuse as a social problem in Ireland in the early 70's is illustrated by an early piece of research which was carried out in 1977 by Sona Smith, a medical social worker, and Patrick Deasy, a paediatrician, in Our Lady's Hospital for Sick Children, in Crumlin, Dublin. Their findings suggested that between 1971 and 1976 child abuse accounted for one in seven hundred admissions to their hospital. They forecast that increased awareness and recognition of the problem would at least double this incidence. In fact, statistics collected by the Department of Health ten years later, in 1983-87 revealed that the number of confirmed cases now being recognised had not simply doubled, it had increased by 500%. (Gilligan 1991).

The first report of the Committee on Non-Accidental Injury was published in 1976, and this represented the basis for all subsequent guidelines issued by the Department of Health. Early reactions to this report by organisations such as the Irish Association of Social Workers were critical of its over-concentration on the detection of physical signs of child maltreatment, and its neglect of the emotional, psychological and social dimensions of child abuse. There was also criticism both of the emphasis on detection at the expense of longer term management, and the absence of plans to develop prevention and intervention skills. The first edition of national child abuse guidelines was published in 1977, known as the Memorandum on Non-Accidental Injury to Children. A later edition was published in 1980, followed by another revised version in 1983. The 1983 guidelines had been preceded by the first investigation into child abuse in Ireland. This had been rather low-key examination into the deaths of two children who were on social workers' caseloads which had identified lack of cohesion, poor communication and lack of coordination in the child protection services. At the same time, however, the investigation report acknowledged the inadequacies of the system. The 1983 guidelines again concentrated mainly on physical abuse, but included 'injury resulting from sexual abuse' in the definitions of child abuse offered.

The number of reported cases of child sexual abuse increased dramatically during the mid eighties, accompanied by the beginnings of considerable media attention on the issue. McKeown and Gilligan (1991) trace the first indication of professional concern with this problem in Ireland to a multi-disciplinary seminar in Incest, organised by the Irish Association of Social Workers in 1983; an outcome of this meeting was a recognition of the need for an Irish study on child sexual abuse. In 1984, the Irish Council for Civil Liberties set up a Working Party on Child Sexual Abuse, whose brief was 'to gather data, to review existing policies, services and laws concerning child sexual abuse and to make specific recommendations'. (Cooney and Torode 1989). The report of the working party, published in 1989 and edited by Tom Cooney and Ruth Torode, was informed by a number of research studies specially commissioned, a review of recent studies and statistics, and consultation visits to other countries. The working party was aware that child sexual abuse was 'defined differently in different cultures and contexts in ways which either lack precision or applicability'(p.2) and sought to explore the problem in an Irish context, taking account of features specific to it, which impacted on the way the problem was understood and addressed. The studies which were commissioned by the working party were themselves affected by the fact that in 1984, the existence of child sexual abuse was barely recognised in Ireland, and there was no ready access to victims which obviously limited the researchers.

The ICCL report highlighted how the way in which child sexual abuse was perceived in Ireland was affected by a number of pertinent issues. 'Unresolved moral questions in Irish society which appear too threatening to or divisive to debate freely and rationally' were reflected, according to the authors, in many of the obstacles to adequately addressing the problem, such as late disclosure, inadequate legal and social responses, lack of resources and professional discomfort. The dearth of sex education programmes at the time, together with what the authors describe as 'anxiety about moral and sexual norms in Ireland' did little to invite the type or level of public discussion which would be necessary to raise awareness and initiate responses to victims, who were socially inhibited from seeking help.

Cooney and Torode also alluded to the particular position of the family in Ireland, pointing to the constitutional position of (married) parents in relation to children which resulted in a lack of child-centredness. The patriarchal nature of family life, in their view, was reflected in the legitimated domination of husbands of their wives, which was 'being eroded only in piecemeal fashion'(p.13). They considered that the way in which the legal system operated also acted as an obstacle to successful prosecutions of sex offenders, due to the particular evidential and procedural requirements of the courts.

Professionals factors which, in the view of the Working Party, acted as constraints to effective action included insufficient support for voluntary and self-help groups, and their lack of integration with professional services; lack of information and training on the subject, and the assumption in official guidance that child sexual abuse could be dealt with adequately in the same fashion as non-accidental injury. The Working Party Report also criticised the *ad hoc* fashion in which funding was contracted to voluntary bodies to provide services, without specification of the type or quality of work expected. This, they considered, led at times to divergence in standards and poor coordination. Amongst their recommendations, they included the implementation of mandatory reporting of child sexual abuse, co-ordinated provision of child care services nationally which might ensure standardisation of responses to child abuse referrals. They also suggested improvements in the management of case conferences, the establishment of a central register for suspected and confirmed cases of child sexual abuse, and the provision of adequate treatment services for adults and children. The lack of a knowledge base which could usefully be applied in an Irish context was particularly noted by the working party, who felt that the need to rely on international research findings ignored some of the contextual realities and particular demographic factors which needed to be considered in relation to Irish children who may be at risk of sexual abuse.

Many of the reforms which were advocated by the ICCL Working Party were also recommended in the Law Reform Commission *Report on Child Sexual Abuse* (1990). The issue of mandatory reporting was again discussed, with recommendations concerning case conferences and child abuse registers. The Law Reform Commission introduced, for the first time in Irish policy or guidance about child protection, the stipulation that the Gardai (the Irish police force) should be involved in the 'early stages' of investigation of child sexual abuse, in order to facilitate the possibility of a prosecution. In a similar legalistic vein, they strongly recommended the empowerment of the Health Boards to seek *ex parte* barring orders in order to remove abusers from the home (which has finally come to fruition in the Domestic Violence Act 1996). In keeping with these reforms, the LRC suggested a re-vamping of the court system to render it more 'child-friendly', and the introduction of a special panel of suitable solicitors with the availability of special information and training to the judiciary.

These important documents reflect the growing awareness of child sexual abuse in Ireland in the 1980's. This had its origins in the way the problem was being re-framed internationally, and depended for its acceptance and expansion on the work of voluntary associations and pressure groups such as the Irish Association of social workers, the Incest Crisis Service and the Rape Crisis Centre. The Department of Health signalled an acknowledgment of the problem by its allocation of funding for research and for the establishment of services. (McKeown and Gilligan 1991). These developments must also be viewed in the context of legal changes which had been on the way for a number of years, starting with their conception in the Task Force on Child Care Services, and finally coming to fruition in the form of the Child Care Act 1991.

The most recent edition of Irish child abuse guidelines, which follows the 1983 version, was published in 1987. For the first time, the Department of Health guidelines gave a comprehensive definition of abuse as: 'physical injuries, severe neglect and sexual or emotional abuse'. The title had significantly changed to *Child Abuse Guidelines*, abandoning for the first time the concept of child abuse as consisting exclusively of 'non-accidental injury'. The importance of inter-agency and inter-professional work was emphasised, and the centrality of case conferences underlined. For the first time, the roles and responsibilities of all professionals in the child protection network were outlined.

During the 1980's, the numbers of reported child abuse allegations rose steadily. At the end of 1978, the total incidence of 'non-accidental injury to children' for the previous 21 months was 243. A decade later in 1988, the total number of reports for the year was 2,673, reflecting a more than ten-fold increase. In the meantime, the Child Care and Protection Bill 1985 evolved into the Child Care Bill 1988, and finally the Child Care Act 1991 was signed into law by President Robinson in 1991. In keeping with the 'genteel pace of reform' (Gilligan 1992-93) the implementation of the new legislation was phased over several years, the final sections having been implemented in December 1996.

The Child Care Act 1991

The Child Care Act 1991 is the first piece of legislation in Ireland to deal with children in a comprehensive manner. The Children Act 1908 had been drafted at a time when social services as we know them did not exist, and its main provisions were concerned with offences against children and offences by children (Greene 1979). The Child Care Act 1991, for the first time, clarifies the role, duties and powers of the Health Boards. In addition to specifying the Health Boards' obligations to protect children in emergencies and provide and review satisfactory arrangements for those who are admitted to 'care', the act sanctions Health Boards 'to promote the welfare of children in its area'. Essentially, then the underlying philosophy of the act is pro-active, and the Health Boards are required to 'have regard to the principle that it is generally in the best interests of a child to be brought up in his or her own family'. In common with British leglisation, the Child Care Act 1991 reflects the 'competing discourses' of treatment and punishment (Merrick 1996), and essentially expects practitioners to walk the delicate tightrope between giving primacy to the protection of children and minimising state intervention into family life. In practice, it remains to be seen whether the welfare principles underpinning the act will counter-balance the more surveillance and 'risk' oriented discourse that has been emerging internationally (Parton 1991, 1996) and in Ireland (Buckley, Skehill and O'Sullivan 1996).

The Child Care Act 1991 started its slow establishment in 1991. The first two sections, empowering the Minister to bring the provisions of the act into effect, and defining a 'child' as a person up to eighteen years old, were implemented in 1991 along with a smaller subsection which concerned the selling of solvents. In late 1992, further sections were implemented. These obliged the Health Boards to promote the welfare of children by providing a range of child care and family support services, and also empowered the Boards to receive children into voluntary care and required them to provide accommodation for homeless children. However, the sections dealing with protection of children in emergencies, the taking of care proceedings and regulations around the placement of children in care were not implemented for a further three years. The procrastination which resulted in so many years of the Act remaining 'in the pipeline' rather than becoming operational appeared to have its roots in political inertia. (O'Sullivan 1995, O'Connor 1992). The main impetus for its implementation eventually emanated from a child abuse inquiry which was described by Ferguson (1993/94) as a 'powerful symbolic event' which focused public and political interest on the subject of child abuse.

The Kilkenny incest investigation

The 'Kilkenny' case as it became known, concerned the sexual and physical abuse of a young woman by her father over many years. The notoriety surrounding the case arose out of media reports of the father's trial and sentencing for incest. It became known that the health and social services had had over one hundred contacts with the family in the thirteen years prior to the prosecution, during which time the abuse had continued. The television coverage of the case included an interview with the young woman, known by the pseudonym of 'Mary', in which she criticised the social worker involved. In the wake of further widespread condemnation of the child care services, the Minister for Health announced a public inquiry, the first of its kind in Ireland. The inquiry team, under the chairpersonship of a judge, Catherine McGuinness, reported after three months. The report identified a number of deficiencies in both the child protection system, and in the professional activities of the various practitioners involved particularly in relation to poor inter-agency cooperation, weaknesses in management and 'lack of the necessary effective probing' (p.88). However, like several British inquiries (London Borough of Brent 1985, Butler Sloss 1988) the investigating team went beyond their original brief to comment on the 'ambivalence of the community as a whole to this type of violence' (p.89). They also acknowledged the complexity involved in determining the boundaries between personal autonomy and State intervention, the preservation of the balance between the rights of individual and family privacy, and 'the duty of the State or society to intervene in situations of moral danger or abuse'. In that sense, the inquiry did not seek to vilify or scapegoat any individuals, and the 'Kilkenny case' was set firmly within its social context. While the report made very specific recommendations for improvements in the child protection system, the inquiry team acknowledged that

> Procedures in themselves whether statutory or otherwise, are not a substitute for good practice, and services must be responsive to local circumstances and resources must be available to ensure that intervention is effective (p.97).

The recommendations of the Report of the Kilkenny Incest Investigation were broad in their attempts to address the issue of child abuse, but they were limited to the extent that they emanated from a retrospective study of the events surrounding one case. Child abuse inquiries, while valuable in themselves, ignore the contextual realities in which child protection practice is situated, and it is questionable whether or not an inquiry provides a suitable theoretical foundation for the design of a set of general principles aimed at governing professional practice. (*See* Buckley 1996a) However, child protection policy making in Ireland has tended to follow high profile happenings in a political, piecemeal fashion, (McGrath 1996) and for this time, the Report of the Kilkenny Incest Investigation provided the catalyst needed to progress the child care services. Following its publication, the Minister for Health made a commitment to implement the remaining sections of the Child Care Act 1991, and to this end, pledged a considerable financial investment in the resourcing of new services and the creation of more child care posts. These developments were welcomed, but the parallel public expectation that the problem of child abuse had been firmly dealt with subsequently struck a note of despair in the hearts of many child protection practitioners (Buckley, Skehill and O'Sullivan 1996).

Child abuse guidelines in Ireland: For whose protection ?
One of the inevitable consequences of the Kilkenny case, and the other child abuse scandals which followed, has been the tightening up of procedural guidance for child protection practitioners. These relate to a number of professions. The role of schools in the identification, investigation and management of child abuse was emphasised in the Report of the Kilkenny Incest Investigation, which firmly endorsed the implementation of the child abuse guidelines for teachers which had been in operation since the early 1990's.[1]

The Kilkenny report had also drawn attention to the need for a smooth flow of information between the police and the Health Boards, and recommended the introduction of an agreed policy for effective inter-agency communication. Work which had already been in progress between the Departments of Health and Justice culminated in the publication in April 1995 of a set of procedures outlining the necessary steps in joint notification of child abuse between the Irish police force - the Gardai - and the Health Boards.[2]

In addition, the Report of the Kilkenny Incest Investigation recommended the introduction of mandatory reporting. In doing so, it endorsed previous calls by the Irish Council for Civil Liberties, (1988) and the Law Reform Commission (1990). Scandals in the Catholic Church, involving 'paedophile priests' revealed that a number of child abuse allegations had been made against members of the Church over the past number of years. Some of these had received a response, albeit muted, but it was discovered that in other cases, the Archbishop had paid out large sums of money to compensate the victims of members of the clergy. In a number of cases, the statutory authorities had never been informed of these cases, and in some instances, the priests involved had been moved to other areas where they once again had access to children. Following immense media exposure of the subject, a working party was formed to address the problem of sexual abuse by clergy and members of religious orders, and in January 1996, a set of guidelines was published, which included an undertaking by the Catholic Church to report all suspicions of abuse to the Health Boards[3].

In practice, all these guidelines and procedures have been implemented. However, their effectiveness is debatable and continues to raise doubts about the feasibility of imposing technical solutions to an area as complex as child abuse. For example, a study in the North West of Ireland on the role of teachers in child abuse (Kelly 1996) indicates that there is a high level of ambiguity about the following of procedures, and that teachers process their concerns about child abuse in different ways, not all within the official system. This ambiguity is seen to stem from a 'less than clear societal mandate to carry out their caring role towards children' (p. 84).

The usefulness of the 1995 guidelines for the *Notification of Suspected Child Abuse between the Health Boards and the Gardai* is also questionable, given the hurried manner in which they became operational. The implementation of these procedures represented a move towards the improvement of inter-agency co-operation, but were introduced with no preparatory training and without any structural arrangements to facilitate the joint work which they prescribed. Previous research on police/social work relations in Ireland (Buckley 1993) had highlighted many of the reasons for poor co-operation between the two organisations. Principal among these were the lack of any arrangements for communication; there were no designated Gardai to deal with cases of child abuse, record-keeping was poor, and differing shift patterns caused delays in contact. A reluctance to co-operate emanated from the stereotypical images each agency had of the other; the social workers perceived the Gardai as 'insensitive' 'poorly educated', and having 'chips on their shoulders' while the Gardai saw the social workers as 'do-gooders', 'useless', 'anti-police' and 'over the top about confidentiality'. Research carried out since the implementation of the procedures indicates that many of the previously identified problems remain (Buckley, Skehill and O'Sullivan 1996). While there is evidence that in the UK, relationships between social workers and police have considerably improved within a context of specialisation and training (Hallett 1995) there is no indication of any commitment to building a similar infra-structure in Ireland.

The debate on mandatory reporting in Ireland is ongoing. In February 1996, in response to many public calls for its introduction, the Minister for Health published a discussion document entitled *'Putting Children First',* and invited submissions from interested parties. Although the concept received much support from politicians, working parties, and prominent child care agencies over the years, responses to the discussion document illustrated a certain retraction of earlier convictions. For example, the Commission on Justice and Peace, a working party set up by the Catholic Bishops, compared the introduction of mandatory reporting to the imposition of a 'straitjacket'[4].

Papers presented at a consultative forum to discuss the issue indicated[5] that prominent professional associations such as the Irish Hospital Consultants' Association were opposed to mandatory reporting. While most voluntary child care agencies support its introduction, the statutory agencies, such as the Health Boards and the Probation and Welfare service, have advised a much more measured approach, and advocated a strong re-inforcement of the system, followed by a trial period before the reporting of child abuse is placed on a legal footing.

Policy in relation to child protection in Ireland observes a certain rhetoric, and contains assumptions about the wisdom and efficacy of following a particular line. On the one hand, child protection practice to date has escaped the bureaucratic and cumbersome requirements imposed in some other European countries, particularly the UK (see Pringle 1997 this volume) but at the same time, in many ways, policy makers have failed to take due account of the position faced on a daily basis by practitioners at the front-line. It has already pointed out that new initiatives in child protection policy have tended to be politically driven, rather than emerging from the recommendations of empirical research, and there is strong evidence that, in the process, they lack a certain amount of realism and applicability. The following section will report on research studies carried out in the Irish context over the past three years which illustrate the true nature day to day child protection practice in statutory settings.

Current child protection practice in Ireland:
Messages from research
The response to child abuse and neglect reports

An in-depth study on child protection in one local authority (Health Board) area was carried out by this author shortly after the implementation of the second part of the Child Care Act 1991, (requiring the Health Boards to promote the welfare of children) and the publication of the Report of the Kilkenny Incest Investigation. (Buckley 1996b). The study was exploratory in nature, and sought to qualitatively examine the response of a team of social workers to child abuse and neglect referrals. This research served to highlight the disparity between the 'official' discourse of child protection in Ireland, as illustrated in the law, child care policies, child abuse guidelines and local procedures. It challenged a number of core assumptions inherent in the version of child protection which is claimed to frame practice in the statutory services in Ireland.The first such assumption is that child protection social workers follow the sort of rational line of action outlined in official procedures when processing child abuse allegations. The study showed that in practice, several criteria operated to consistently filter referrals out of the system prior to official investigation. One was a 'civil rights' ideal, whereby the social workers were concerned about unnecessarily 'confronting' families as they saw it - intervening in family privacy. This was closely associated with the second main criterion used - the belief that child abuse investigations often did more harm than good, particularly where parents were vulnerable, lacking in confidence and needed a different type of response. The research showed that instead of automatically entering reports into the system, thereby starting the unstoppable process of investigation, social workers tended to delay action until they could somehow informally or quietly check out the situation without necessarily involving other professionals or even speaking to the family themselves. This process, which in reality breached the child abuse guidelines, satisfied the social workers that they were not taking precipitate action. It also had the advantage of keeping the numbers of investigations at a more manageable level.

The second assumption underlying the official version of child protection in Ireland which was questioned by this study was the willingness of all child care professionals to assume a role in child protection, or to coordinate that role with the statutory services. It has already been shown that the issue of inter-agency and inter-professional coordination was the focus of much concern in the child abuse inquiry reports. Efforts to improve it were seen to be crucial in ensuring an efficient child protection system, but these endeavours consisted mainly of exhortations or protocols stipulating co-operation rather than making any effort to unpack and address the underlying impediments. The inadequacy of this approach was borne out in the research which indicated, at each stage in the careers of cases, barriers to the communication of child abuse concerns between professionals outside and inside the statutory system: different perceptions of roles and responsibilities, differing professional orientations, lack of trust in the system, fear of over-zealous and insensitive interventions, disagreement about ethical norms such as confidentiality, and sometimes ignorance about way the child protection system worked. Reporting behaviour was very inconsistent, and there were instances where general practitioners, Gardai, non-statutory welfare officers and private therapists reported child abuse, but failed to supply the Health Boards with the contextual information needed to facilitate investigation of the allegations. Many of these referrals were made with ambivalence and almost distaste, reporters not wanting to be identified, or to involve themselves in any depth. In several instances the reporters dropped out of contact before completing the referrals.

The problems with inter-agency and inter-professional coordination were closely connected with a third assumption challenged by this study, that case conferences and other inter-agency meetings such as child abuse reviews, which are given such a central position in the machinery of child protection, are effective fora for decision making. In reality, while case conferences were considered useful and beneficial at times, there was strong evidence to show that the powerful interactional processes at these meetings tended to deflect energy and attention away from the interests of families and children, and that interventions were frequently planned around inter-agency conflicts rather than focused on the presenting risks or concerns of the families involved.

The key point in this study has been the contrast between the reality of child protection practice which is exposed when these activities are seen in context, and the desire for 'certainty' which is creeping into the public and managerial perception and expectations about what is achievable to address child abuse in Ireland. It would be fair to say at this stage that the way the official discourse is now being fashioned is a cause of despair to many practitioners, who feel that most of the time, attention is being focused on the wrong issues, and resources are misplaced by an over-concentration on investigation. This latter point was strongly borne out by a later study, commissioned by a Health Boards and carried out in 1996 (Buckley, Skehill and O'Sullivan 1996).

The Buckley, Skehill and O'Sullivan (1996) study looked retrospectively at the 'intake' to social work teams in a Health Boards area over a two month period, and collected a certain amount of quantitative data in order to provide the context for a later qualitative study of a sample of cases over a six month period. It was discovered that most clients who were referred to the social work service had, as well as the reason for referral, a number of family 'problems' or 'crises' in common. The most common were 'immature parenting' 'behavioural problems in children' 'parental illness' 'financial problems'. However, the study indicated that the strongest response was made to those families whose major reason for referral concerned child abuse and neglect. Intervention in these cases was accountable at several levels, and decisions were made at inter-disciplinary meetings. Child abuse and neglect cases were twice as likely to be allocated to social workers and offered an ongoing service than those where there was no tangible evidence of risk. Furthermore, while child abuse guidelines and procedures were generally followed, and initial referrals received prompt responses, there was less evidence in the research that plans for ongoing case management were realistically made or reviewed, or that treatment services were adequate.

A striking feature which the two Irish studies just described have in common is the way in which referrals for 'neglect' which have always dominated the child abuse statistics, receive a less concerted response in terms of investigation, ongoing support and intervention than do those which involve sexual or physical abuse.

These two research studies illustrate the way in the Irish child protection system operates in terms of its response to referrals of child abuse and neglect to the statutory services. A most important perspective, however, which has received little official attention, is the concept of partnership with families.

Partnership with families
The Child Care Act 1991 pays a certain amount of attention to the concept of partnership with parents, but really only in terms of their role in the lives of their children in the care of the State. In other respects, the focus of the Act on family support suggests that the main focus of work should be with children in their own families, but that is the extent of its concern with partnership. Likewise, apart from a stipulation to contact parents as soon as possible to discuss the allegations that have arisen about their children, the 1987 *Child Abuse Guidelines* make little reference to parental participation. The Report of the Kilkenny Incest Investigation goes a little further in its recommendation for 'the attendance of parents/guardians at case conferences unless there are substantial grounds for their inclusion'. The 1995 guidelines for *Notification of Cases of Suspected Child Abuse Between the Gardai and the Health Boards* allude to parental participation at case conferences, but in a rather negative tone. In the section on case conferences, (p.14) the procedures point out that

> the practice has developed in some Health Boards areas of inviting the parent(s) of the child to participate ... to avoid misunderstanding, a Health Boards should inform the Gardai where this is the practice in its area.

The emphasis here seems to be on the protection of professionals against any disruption that this may cause. Parental participation in the child protection process is therefore, dependent on the discretion of local managers. The study carried out by Buckley, Skehill and O'Sullivan (1996) in a local authority area revealed that while social workers aspired towards partnership with parents, there was little evidence of it happening in practice, particularly in the early stages of investigation and planning. Parental participation at case conferences was extremely low, and only partial when it did happen. Interviews with the parents themselves strongly illustrated their feelings of exclusion, and frustration. The majority of them voiced the desire to fully participate in case conferences and contribute to the discussion process. Those who had attended the end of case conferences for 'feedback' found the experience to be humiliating, and embarrassing, reflecting poor commitment on the part of professionals towards a policy of inclusion. While the notion of partnership inherent in the British legislation is regarded somewhat cynically at times by those who equate it with the right wing aspiration towards 'growth in personal responsibility, independence and individual choice' (Howe 1996), its absence in Irish child protection policy can be shown to have a detrimental effect on working relationships. The earlier study by Buckley (1996b) illustrated that parents felt very distanced from the child protection services, and often perceived their own needs very differently from the way that groups of practitioners did. The shock of being investigated, and devastation at finding that their children had been abused by, for example, a trusted family member, often combined to create huge barriers between parents and services. The lack of opportunity to voice their needs and contribute to planning frequently meant that these impediments remained, and greatly reduced the prospects of rehabilitation. Additionally, parents in the Buckley, Skehill and O'Sullivan study, while generally satisfied with the services offered to their children, had a perception that they themselves were not being offered anything. Many of them were short of money, depressed, isolated from family and friends, and some had been subject to violence from their partners. What to them appeared to be a child (abuse) centred service, ignored their own needs and offered little support to their parenting.

The gendered nature of the Irish child protection system
The limited research available on child protection in the Irish context suggests that the way in which child abuse reports are processed reflects a 'gendered' practice. Replicating the findings of Farmer and Owen (1995) and Gibbons, Conroy and Bell (1995) in the British context, research in Ireland illustrates the tendency of the child protection system to focus on mothers, even when the alleged abuser is the father, or partner of the mother (Buckley 1996b). The exhortations of the Child Care Act 1991 to provide a range of support services to families further reinforce the notion that responsibility for child care rests mainly with women. Family support work, like other home-based services such as foster care, is regarded as a superior option to those which are institutionally based. These services are usually

provided by women, usually on a part-time basis, and directed at women (Opgenhaffen 1996). Their cheapness adds greatly to their appeal to service providers. The Community Mothers Programme 'of low key domiciliary parent education and support to mothers with young children' (Gilligan 1996) is probably the most widespread model of family support that is being adopted throughout the country. This programme is delivered by women in the same communities as the families they are serving, and is supervised by Health Board public health nurses. While it has been evaluated as bringing significant gains to particpating mothers and their children (Johnson and Molloy 1995) it certainly does not challenge the feminisation of child care work. The absence of fathers from 'sites of support' such as play groups and family centres reinforces this configuration (Murphy 1996).

Similarly, other front-line child protection services are carried out by a predomi-nantly female workforce of social workers, public health nurses, and community care child care workers. The latter two professions are entirely female. In 1996, 85% of the social workers in the Midland and Mid-West, two of the eight Health Boards, were female (Doherty 1996). In contrast, just under half of the statutory social work managers in the Republic are male (Department of Health 1996).

Those whom an administrator recently referred to as 'ordinary carers' actually carry responsibility for the care and protection of 74% of the children in the care of the State. (Doherty 1996). These foster carers are, for the most part, two parent families, but in the traditional fashion, most mothers in foster families are only able to carry out their fostering roles by virtue of their unemployed and available status. For their efforts, they are paid £2,500 to £3,500 each year, compared to the average £38,000 and up to £50,000 it is now estimated to cost to keep a child in residential care[6].

Child protection in families where violence is committed against mothers
Recent research has confirmed that a high level of violence is committed by men against women in Ireland. Kelleher and Associates and O'Connor (1995) showed in their study that 18% of Irish women, surveyed on a national basis, have been subjected to violence including physical injury. The same survey showed that 64% of women who experienced violence reported that their children had witnessed it happening. The effects on their children included poor school performance, the children becoming fearful and withdrawn, and experiencing sleeping problems. 'Exposure to domestic violence' was included in the definitions of child abuse

offered by the Minister for Health in the discussion document on mandatory reporting (Department of Health 1996). Yet, as the Kelleher *et al* research showed, violence against women in the home has not been identified as a special issue in need of attention by the social work service, nor, according to the study, was violence against women in the home part of in-service training for social workers. An earlier study by Killion (1993) highlighted the 'artificial separation' between social workers' professional responsibility for the welfare of children, and their responsibility for the welfare and safety of their mothers. Women reported to the study how they tended to deny to social workers that their children were subjected to physical abuse by their partners, mainly out of fear of losing them, and in the process 'paved a way out for the social worker' to withdraw from the case. The same study reflected mothers' views that even though their ability to parent was diminished as a result of being battered and abused, the response they received from social workers was unsatisfactory and unhelpful. Refuge staff complained that social workers had very limited knowledge about the effects of violence upon children.

Cultural relativism in Irish child protection work

Unlike some other European countries, Irish society is not multi-racial, nor does it have a high immigration rate. However, the concept of 'cultural relativism' (Dingwall, Eekelaar and Murray 1983)[7] is applicable in relation to the Travelling community. Child abuse reports concerning the small sample of Travellers in the study by Buckley (1996b) received quite a different response to those from the settled population. Unless there was a compelling reason for the Health Board to intervene, such as one occasion when a child was literally abandoned, the investigation of child abuse allegations about Travellers was left to the police. Because of the rigid boundaries between catchment areas and the mobility of the Travellers, families where there were child protection concerns were unlikely to be consistently followed up by the same team of social workers, and no service was prepared to take overall responsibility for coordinating interventions. A study by O'Higgins (1993) which focused on the families of Traveller children in care illustrated the high level of childhood adversity suffered by them. The research revealed that in comparison to the settled population, Traveller children were overrepresented among children placed in substitute care, and that the risk of their being admitted to care was greater than for other children. Health-wise, Traveller children are many times more likely to die as a result of road accidents, to suffer from metabolic and congenital defects, and to die pre-natally. The risk is considerably higher in 'unhoused' as opposed to housed Travellers. Despite the fact that a higher number of Traveller children come to the notice of social workers than those of settled families, O'Higgins found that very few received family support or casework services. Similarly, the study by Kelleher and Associates and O'Connor (1995) found that Traveller mothers who were battered by their partners, and by association, Traveller children who were subjected to emotional abuse, had a lot of difficulty engaging the social services.

The future of child protection in Ireland

Before looking to the future, the current situation must first of all be appraised. The above research findings combine to highlight a number of points about child protection practice in Ireland. Firstly, the response to child welfare concerns appears to be framed very much in terms of child abuse and the more tangible aspects of physical neglect. Even within this context, there still appears to exist a strong resistance by professionals to intervene into the private domain of the Irish family. This type of practice still carries traces of the traditional Catholic ethos which resists State interference, and this resistance is made all the more visible by the reluctance of many professionals outside the statutory services to identify with the 'dirty work' of child protection. Despite the pro-active orientation of the Child Care Act 1991, much of the work is 'reactive' and partnership with families operates at quite a low level. In the main, child abuse and the system which deals with it are deemed to be the responsibility of women, and the problem of domestic violence is not given a significant place on the child protection agenda. Adversities which are suffered by children, but do not fall within the 'norm' of child abuse, or do not carry visible evidence of injury, maltreatment or neglect, elicit a weak and sometimes uninformed response from the social services. All this must be set, however, in the context of a developing and expanding child protection system, which has undergone an almost complete metamorphosis in the past decade, and there is every reason to believe that events of the last few years have indeed 'made a difference' in a way that can be framed quite positively.

Certain positive moves have been made. In recognition of the lack of child-centredness in the current child protection system, the Report of the Kilkenny Incest Investigation (McGuinness 1993) referred to the matter of children's rights, recommending that the Government give consideration to the amendment of

Constitution to include a statement of the constitutional rights of children. Prominent child care organisations have also supported this issue. This growing interest in the rights of the child has been supported by Ireland's ratification in 1992 of the United Nations Convention on the Rights of the Child. The *Children's Rights Alliance* was founded in 1993 in order to promote the implementation of the UN convention's in Irish laws, polices and services as they relate to children. Its recently published report has recommended the establishment of a body to 'ensure that the voice of children as heard in the policy and administrative process' and 'help to create an environment more favourable to the protection of children's rights (Cousins 1996).

The recent 'politicisation' (Ferguson 1996) of child abuse in Ireland has put a lot of pressure on the heavily over-burdened system, but has raised public awareness to the degree that child abuse is now a difficult concept to ignore. The aftermath of the 'scandals' of the past few years has been constructive to the extent that it has accelerated the progression of services. The requirement of the Child Care Act 1991 on Health Boards to undertake regular reviews of the adequacy of their child and family services should maintain a level of public accountability to the maintenance of these developments. The widely publicised debate about mandatory reporting has kept child abuse on the social agenda and has provided a platform upon which many current dilemmas about the system are discussed and brought to a wide audience. Likewise, the growing body of literature and research concerning the state of child protection in Ireland will continue to highlight the deficits in service provision and the concerns of practitioners and policy makers.

As well as research on the subject, training in child protection has taken on a new impetus over the past few years. In addition to mainstream social work courses, training for teachers, Gardai, doctors, nurses and most professions who come into contact with children now contain components which will add to their knowledge about how to identify child abuse and how to act on their concerns. Training in child protection at a post-qualifying multi-disciplinary level is taking place in two Irish universities, and most Health Boards have now begun to address this issue on a local basis.

It also has to be remembered that despite the failures and mistakes which are only too obvious in the Irish child protection system, the ever-growing child abuse statistics also reflect the growth in child protection activity. Seen in these terms, the work can be viewed positively, and when it is placed in a historical, or even recent, perspective, it can be seen that Irish society has gone to greater lengths than ever before to make provision for the protection of its children.

Notes

[1] *Procedures for Dealing with Allegations or Suspicions of Child Abuse* Department of Education 1991

[2] *Notification of Suspected Cases of Child Abuse between the Gardai and the Health Boardss.* Department of Health 1995

[3] *Child Sexual Abuse: Framework for a Church Response.* Report of the Irish Catholic Bishops' Advisory Committee on Child Sexual Abuse by Priests and Religious

[4] *Mandatory Reporting of Child Abuse: Safeguards and Rights.* The Irish Commission for Justice and Peace

[5] *The Reporting of Child Abuse - The Contribution of Mandatory reporting* hosted by the Minister of State for Children, Austin Currie TD on 16th September 1996

[6] Approximate costings given by Child Care Services, Eastern Health Board in September 1996

[7] Dingwall (1989) defines 'cultural relativism' as 'a "get out" clause which can be used to reduce the importance of less than desirable behaviour by pointing to alternative standards which may allow the behaviour to be judged "good enough"'. The example he uses is the justification of West Indian parents beating their children by seeing such treatment as the reflection of a traditional use of physical punishment in the community

References

Beckford Report, *A Child in Trust,* The report of the panel of inquiry into the death of Jasmine Beckford, London: London Borough of Brent, 1985.

Breen, R., Hannan, D., Rottman, D., Whelan, T. *Understanding Contemporary Ireland: State, Class and Development in the Republic of Ireland.* Gill and Macmillan, 1990.

Buckley, H. 'The Kilkenny Incest Investigation: Some Practice Implications' *Irish Social Worker,* Vol.11, No.4,1993.

Buckley, H. 'Child Abuse Guidelines in Ireland: For Whose Protection? *Administration* Vol.44 No.2, 1996.

Buckley, H. *Beyond the Rhetoric: A qualitative study of child protection in Ireland,* Paper presented to the ISPCAN Congress, Dublin, August 1996

Buckley, H., Skehill, C. and O'Sullivan, E. *An Overview of Child Protection Practices in the South Eastern Health Board,* 1996.

Butler-Sloss, Lord Justice E. *Report of the Inquiry into Child Abuse in Cleveland in 1987,* London, HMSO, 1988.

Campaign Group for the Development of Personal Social Services *The Future of Personal Social Services in Health Boards, Eastern Health Board, 1983*

Committee on Reformatory and Industrial Schools, *Report on the Reformatory and Industrial School System*: Dublin Stationery Office, 1970.

Cooney, T. and Torode, R. *Irish Council for Civil Liberties Working Party on Child Sexual Abuse Report 1989.* Dublin: ICCL.

Cousins, M. *Seen and Heard: Promoting and Protecting Children's Rights in Ireland.* The Children's Rights Alliance - Republic of Ireland, 1996.

Department of Education *Procedures for Dealing with Allegations or Suspicions of Child Abuse.* Dublin: Department of Education, 1991.

Department of Health *Guidelines for Development of Social Work Services (In Community Care Programme)* 1973.

Department of Health, *Report of Committee on Non-Accidental Injury to Children:* Dublin, Stationery Office, 1976.

Department of Health, *Memorandum on Non Accidental Injury to Children* Dublin, Stationery Office,1977.

Department of Health, *Non-Accidental Injury to Children. Guidelines on Procedures for the Identification, Investigation and Management of Non-Accidental Injury to Children* Dublin: Department of Health, 1980.

Department of Health, *Task Force on Child Care Services: Final Report* Dublin: Stationery Office, 1981.

Department of Health, *Non-Accidental Injury to Children: Guidelines on Procedures for the Identification, Investigation and Management of Non-Accidental Injury to Children* Dublin: Department of Health, 1983

Department of Health, *Child Abuse Guidelines: Guidelines on Procedures for the Identification, Investigation and Management of Child Abuse* Dublin: Department of

Health, 1987.

Department of Health, *Notification of Suspected Cases of Child Abuse between the Health Boards and the Gardai* Dublin: Department of Health, 1995.

Department of Health *Child Abuse Statistics 1987-1993)* 1995

Department of Health, *Putting Children First: a Discussion Document on Mandatory Reporting of Child Abuse* Dublin: Department of Health, 1996.

Department of Health, *Directory of Social Work Managers in the Health Board Community Care Teams.* 1996

Dingwall, R., Eekelaar, J., Murray, T., *The Protection of Children: State Intervention and Family Life.* Oxford: Blackwell, 1983.

Dingwall, R. (1989) 'Labelling Children as Abused or Neglected' in W.Stainton Rogers, Hevey, D. and Ash, E., *Child Abuse and Neglect: Facing the Challenge,* London: Batsford 1989.

Doherty, D., 'Child Care and Protection: Protecting the Children - Supporting Their Service Providers' *Administration Vol.44No.2,* 1996.

Farmer, E. and Owen, M. *Child Protection Practice: Private Risks and Public Remedies* London: HMSO, 1995.

Ferguson, H., Gilligan, R., Torode R., (eds.) *Surviving Childhood Adversity: Issues for Policy and Practice,* Dublin: Social Studies Press, 1993.

Ferguson, H., 'Surviving Irish Childhood: Child Protection and the Death of Children in Child Abuse Cases in Ireland since 1884 in *Surviving Childhood Adversity: Issues for Policy and Practice.* op.cit.

Ferguson, H. 'Child Abuse Inquiries and the Report of the Kilkenny Incest Investigation: A Critical Analysis' in *Administration,* Vol.41 (Winter 1993-4)

Ferguson, H., 'Protecting Irish Children in Time: Child Abuse as a Social Problem and the Development of the Child Protection System in the Republic of Ireland' in *Administration* vol.44, No.2, 1996.

Gibbons, J. Conroy, S, and Bell, C. *Operating the child protection system: A study of child protection practices in English local authorities* HMSO, 1995.

Gilligan, R. *Irish Child Care Services: Policy, Practice and Provision.* Institute of Public Administration, 1991.

Gilligan, R. 'The Child Care Act 1991: An Examination of its Scope and Resource Implications' *Administration* Vol.40 No.4, 1992/3.

Gilligan, R. 'Irish Child Care Services in the 1990's' *Child Welfare Services: Developments in Law, Policy, Practice and Research,* London: Jessica Kingsley, 1996.

Greene, D.'Legal Aspects of Non-Accidental Injury to Children' in *Administration,* Vol.27.No.4, 1979.

Hallett, C. *Inter-Agency Cooperation in Child Protection* London: HMSO, 1995.

Howe, D. 'Surface and depth in social work practice' in *Social Theory, Social Change and Social Work.* London: Routledge, 1996

Irish Catholic Bishops Advisory Committee on Chiild Sexual Abuse by Priests and Religious (1996) *Child Sexual Abuse: Framework for a Church Response*

Irish Association of Social Workers, *Comments on the Report of the Committee on Non Accidental Injury to Children,* 1976.

Johnson, Z and Molloy, B. 'The Community Mothers Programme: empowerment of parents by parents' in *Children and Society* 9,2, 1995.

Kelleher and Associates and O'Connor, *Making the Links: Towards an integrated strategy for the elimination of violence against women in intimate relationships with men.* Dublin: Women's Aid. 1995.

Kempe, H., and Helfer R, *The Battered Child* University of Chicago Press, 1968.

Killion, M. 'Dilemmas in dealing with domestic violence' *Irish Social* Worker Vol.11 No.3, 1993

Law Reform Commission, *Report on Child Sexual Abuse,* Dublin, Law Reform Commission, 1990

McKeown, K. and Gilligan, R., 'Child Sexual Abuse in the Eastern Health Board Region of Ireland in 1988: An Analysis of 512 Confirmed Cases' in *The Economic and Social Review* Vol.22, No.2, 1991.

Merrick, D., *Social Work and Child Abuse* London, Routledge, 1996.

McGrath, K. 'Intervening in Child Sexdual Abuse in Ireland: Towards Victim Centred Policies and Practices' *Administration* Vol.44 No.2, 1996

McGuinness, C. *The Report of the Kilkenny Incest Investigation* Dublin: Stationery Office, 1993.

Milner, J. 'Avoiding Violent Men: The Gendered Nature of Child Protection Policy and Practice' in Ferguson, H., Gilligan, R, and Torode, R. (eds.) *Surviving Childhood Adversity: Issues for Policy and Practice.*, Dublin, Social Studies Press. 1993.

Murphy, M.,'From Prevention to "Family Support" and Beyond: Promoting the Welfare of Irish Children' *Administration,* Vol.44 No.2, 1996.

O'Connor, P. 'Child Care Policy: A Provocative Analysis and Research Agenda' in *Administration,* Vol 40, no.3 (Autumn 1992).

O'Higgins, K. 'Surviving Separation: Traveller Children in Substitute Care' in Ferguson, H., Gilligan, R., and Torode, R. *Surviving Childhood Adversity* op.cit.

O'Sullivan, E. 'Irish Child Care Law - The Origins, Aims and Development of the 1991 Child Care Act' *Childright* (June) No.97, 1993.

Opgenhaffen, R., *The Family - Family Support Worker Relationship- a Study of Five Cases Based on Perceptions of the Family, Family Support Worker and Social Worker.* M.Sc. Thesis, Department of Social Studies, Trinity College, Dublin, 1996.

Parton, N. *Governing the Family: Child Care, Child Protection and the State.* Basingstoke, Macmillan, 1991.

Parton, N. 'Social Work, Risk and the Blaming System *Social Theory, Social Change and Social Work* op.cit., 1996.

Robins, J. *The Lost Children: A Study of Charity Children in Ireland 1700-1900.* Dublin: Institute of Public Administration, 1980.

Senior Social Workers, Eastern Health Board, *Report of Committee on Non Accidental Injury to Children - Senior Social Workers' Comments.* 1976.

Skehill, C., (forthcoming) *Exploring the Nature of Social Work: An Historical Perspective* Occasional Paper Series, Trinity College, Dublin.

Smith, S. and Deasy, P. 'Child Abuse in Ireland' in *The Journal of the Irish Medical Association,* Vol.70 no.3, 1977.
Task Force on Child Care Services, *Final Report,* Dublin: Stationery Office, 1981.

Child Protection in Italy

By Laura Bini and Monica Toselli

Introduction

Two preliminary remarks have to be made when dealing with child protection and its reverse, child maltreatment, in Italy.

First of all every picture of the Italian situation is characterized by striking differences among the three different zones, divided into 22 regions, of the country. The North, Centre and South of Italy although ruled by the same laws present such economic, historical, traditional variations that even the actual policy of child protection has different shapes. We will try to present an adequate picture, to some extent overrepresenting North and Central experiences.

Another remark pertains to child maltreatment. No systematic research can be quoted, there are no precise data of the prevalence of abuse and maltreatment. Also governmental data describing crimes against people do not specify if youngsters are victims of crime, as if child abuse should not be legally and conceptually conceived in different terms from any other abuse. Therefore our analysis will be more centered on the situation of children in a wide context.

The "perception" of childhood as a specific period in the life span is a rapidly changing phenomenon. The problem of defining maltreatment stems from the variability of perceiving particular children's rights and needs. This same perception and sensitivity creates the main criteria for arranging child care. The issue can be considered a problem of social representation (Ventimiglia 1990). Therefore it is meaningful not only to know or infer the "actual" rate of maltreatment in a country more or less realistically, but also to study the different representations of the rate of maltreatment or abuse held by different observers: social workers, researchers, people involved in child care.

After a short sketch about childhood in history, we will deal with the present situation of children and child protection. Subsequently we will present specific acts pertaining to child protection and child protection agencies. The prevailing difficulties in child protection will be described, and a glimpse into the future will be given, stressing future foreseeable problems and future foreseeable ways of overcoming present difficulties.

Children in history

What remains of the past are the most dramatic stories; a picture about childhood can be sketched more through the negative side of relinquished, exploited, maltreated children, than from the positive side of normal children, who are somehow without history.

Italian childhood, from the few documents we have, was as unhappy and maltreated as that in most western countries, as Ariès (1960) has depicted it. This judgement may be antihistorical. Certainly art, literature, documents depict infants looking as sad and suffering as we perceive them in our own time. Children are not represented and cared for as a specific group; they are confused and overwhelmed by adults.

Let us think of the beautiful Giotto Madonnas often holding an infant who is not childish at all, as if even the great painter was unable to look at the real appearance of an infant.

A turning point is therefore represented by the Rennaissance. Exalting men and humanity, the moment came when the specific value of the child was considered. This change can be inferred by the foundation of the first institute devoted only to child care. The misery of childhood could eventually be seen. Until then infants and children, when their parents were unable to take care of them, were abandoned in religious hospitals where sick adults were treated, or in front of the churches. In 1445 (Becchi 1996) the Innocenti Hospital was founded, sponsored by the Arte della Seta, a kind of trade union among florentine silk artisans. In this hospital abandoned children were brought up as future workers. A new building was expressly built by the great architect Filippo Brunelleschi. The first institution in the world just for child care (which now hosts a Unicef Centre for Child Development) shows how a great cultural change (as well as economic interest) could mark a turning point in child care. The beautiful medaillons by Della Robbia, on the porch of the building, represent "childish" looking infants, even if strictly swaddled.

The following centuries were not marked by such a peculiar sensitivity for childhood. Reading Giacomo Casanova's memoirs we can have a sketch of the "normal cruelty" which surrounded a venetian middle class child. The more striking feature is how the particularity of childhood was ignored: children were driven to study or to work like adults.

Literary documents about children's work can be found in Verga's novel "*Rosso Malpelo*" describing the life of little sulphur miners in the XIXth century and in Ledda's novel "*Padre Padrone*" (1970). This last title, whose meaning is "*Father and Master*" describes the life of a child shepherd in Sardinia only 30 years ago.

In order to understand the history of childhood in Italy some words are needed about the influence of the Catholic Church. Until the XIX century every form of care to needy adults and children was administered by religious institutions (apart from particular ones, already cited, like the Innocenti Hospital). The nursing staff were always composed of religious members; care was a religious business. Therefore many positive gains in children's lives, sometimes their survival, are to be attributed to the work and influence of the Church, to her striving for inculcating mercy to suffering people. At the same time, in our opinion, we ought to recognise the powerful influence of the familistic ideology and of the myth of motherhood held by the Catholic Church, in ignoring and denying the phenomenon of maltreatment and sexual abuse inside the family. The worship of the Madonna has always been paralleled by an absolute faith in maternal instinct, which would assure the best care to the child. In an anecdotal way we can quote the saying still used by mothers scolding their children: "I have done you and I will undo you", which documents the absolute ownership of the child that Italian culture attributes to the mother. Another saying, just in the same mood runs "Who has a mother doesn't have to cry".

Catholic associations like the Catholic Association of Italian Workers (A.C.L.I.) have been, in this century, more sensible to another form of child suffering: harshly worked children.

Childhood today

The last governmental report, in 1996, about the condition of childhood tries to propose a positive evaluation of childhood in Italy. Certainly children are becoming more and more rare, the Italian fertility rate (1.2 child per woman) is the lowest in the world. This somehow justifies the fact that social funds for childhood (from 0 to 14 years) are about 1/4 of social funds for elders (see Donati 1991, Shamgar-Handelman 1991 and Cornia 1991 about intergenerational expenses and generational fairness).

We are proud that the award for the best kindergarten in the world, went to one in Reggio Emilia. At the same time not every child who ought to have the right of attending kindergarten can actually attend them (only 5.2 over 100 in 1986, Saraceno 1990).

The infant death rate is rapidly sinking, but it is not yet as low as in most western countries, like France or Denmark. Moreover in Sicily, where we find the highest rate in the whole country it is still 10.2 per 1000 infants born. (Rapporto sulla condizione dell'infanzia in Italia 1996)

School attendance too is a sign of child care and, even though compulsory education entails 8 years of schooling, very high: 10.9% in 1985-86 is the rate of " tension" (Corrado 1989). By tension is meant a mixed index, sum of the rate of school desertion plus school repeating. At the same time a debate is growing about longer schooling, from 8 to 10 years. This aim has not yet been achieved.
Of 100 children attending the first year of secondary school, 90 will finish this education, which, we must remember is compulsory schooling; 72 will go on; only 40 will reach the secondary leaving examination, 26 will attend the university and 8 only will take a degree (Pombeni 1993, p.252). All those youngsters who give up studying try to go and work. The jobs will be more and more unqualified the younger the minors are.

The phenomenon of juvenile work, as we reported above, is still very widespread. Even if the fact that juvenile (less than 14 years old) work has been illegal since a 1961 law (law 1325, and then n.977,1967) has resulted in this data disappearing from governmental statistics, they can still be inferred from the accidents which affect working minors and from the rates of children leaving school. This form of maltreatment (surely related to misery) still affects many children; reasonable estimates consider that in certain zones of southern Italy 20% to 50% of children between 10 and 14 years old are working part time (Saraceno 1991, p.46).
Italian studies very often stress the problem of working children, (see for instance Burgoni, Calanchi, Magri, Pedrazzoli, 1990) explicitly quoting it as a form of

maltreatment. We may wonder if the incidence of the phenomenon is more widespread in our country, due to its economic level, or if there is a particular sensitivity to children's work.

New forms of cruelty in childhood can show up from the attempt to protect children: a recent phenomenon is the use of children as drug pushers since they are not open to prosecution due to their minority. In this sense the data about juvenile delinquency can be read as data about child maltreatment. Minors reported in 1990 for different crimes were 13,341 (Spini 1991). Moreover, it was recently stressed (Rapporto sulla condizione dell'infanzia in Italia 1996) that out of every 4 accused minors, 3 are from southern Italy.

Another way, in our opinion, to observe the welfare of childhood is to check how many children do not live inside their family, being found in different kinds of placements: they are almost 4 out of every 1000 children and represent 7% of all assisted children (Rapporto sulla condizione dei minori in Italia 1996). What has to be stressed, in a positive manner, is that all adoptable children are immediately adopted, without staying more than a few weeks in institutions. This is true for most of disabled children too.

A good "welcome culture" for children in Italy is observable in the fact that a remarkable number of children from zones polluted by the Chernobyl nuclear explosion are regularly received as guests by Italian families for a 30 days period of recovery.

Not to be forgotten is the problem of children in the last few years migrating to Italy from countries outside the European Union. Hard problems of social integration pertain to children coming from Albania, China and those belonging to the Rom and Sinty ethnic cultures, that is gypsies. Everyone of these groups is very marginalized within society even if in different ways.

The Chinese community does not present public order problems; survival is assured exploiting the handicraft work of women and children. Relationships with the wider community are limited since whole families tend to migrate together.

Serious problems come from Albanian organizations which manage trafficking of minors. These organizations survive by exploiting the prostitution of enslaved children, male and female. It is rare that the whole family migrates from Albania to Italy: only children and adolescents are taken in our country for the purpose of prostitution, and here, without doubt, they find clients.

In the two last decades the almost normal cohabitation with gypsy people has become very difficult. Mostly in the last five or ten years the problem of drug abuse and pushing has added to the "ordinary" problems of theft or begging.

In the Rom camps, in the Chinese community, in the Albanian organizations people live wholly marginalized. Only rarely are services acquainted with how children live, even more rarely are they able to intervene. In this case the intervention is usually the removal of the child from his/her community. Many more problems come out from the Rom and Chinese community attempts to recover their children. By contrast Albanian children when removed from their "slave traders" are no longer wanted back by their parents who live far away.

This kind of data highlights the state of childhood in a general way. Let us turn to the few specific data about maltreatment and abuse.

There is no specific observatory about the state of childhood, and the annual report about childhood derives its material from scattered data like, for instance, those pertaining to crimes against minors. Reported crimes are obviously a reduced amount of what in reality happens to children. According to the Conseil d'Europe (1984) the reported cases of rape and abuse are from 5 to 15% of those actually happening. In 1994 there were 2268 prosecuted cases of maltreatment, 77 cases of misuse of punishments and 5 cases of incest (Rapporto sulla condizione dell'infanzia in Italia 1996).

The Italian Association for Prevention of Child abuse estimates that 20000 cases of maltreatment are happening every year, 5000 of which pertain to sexual abuse. (Campanini 1993, p.30)

Research carried out by the research center LABOS on behalf of the Ministry of Justice in 1991 regarding reported crimes against children, stated that, out of 948 cases, 65% related to some kind of sexual abuse, 27% maltreatment of a general nature and 25% injuries (the sum is more than 100 because, as we know, crimes very often cumulate in the same situation). Victims of sexual abuse are mostly females, and mostly (by a factor of two) in the South of Italy, while males are mostly victims of injuries. What emerges is that the number of crimes increases the more the children grow up. We may tentatively consider that what is discovered is only the more visible phenomenon, as maltreatment and abuse in very young children is so difficult to detect. Data which somehow contradict international literature are that crimes in the street happen as often as crimes of this kind inside the victim's and perpetrator's house (L.A.B.O.S.1984-87).

In examining the proceedings of crimes relating to sexual offenses, Ventimiglia (1987) observes that out of 487 proceedings, 61% had minors, boys and girls, as victims.

A narrow window into the phenomenon may be provided by the number of inquires made during the year 1996 about maltreatment and abuse against children in the province of Firenze: out of a population of about 270.000 children (less than 18 years old) just 6 inquires pertained to sexual abuse and 2 to maltreatment (data kindly referred by the Minors department of the Police). Considering that inquires are still one of the first steps in the formal discovery of a crime, it is clear how narrow we may consider these precise data to be in relation to the actual size of the phenomenon.

Data coming from a private centre for studying and intervening in child maltreatment (Centro per il Bambino Maltrattato, (C.B.M.) of Milano) stress that, in the centre experience, out of 100 cases of maltreatment 10 pertain to sexual abuse and 90 to maltreatment as such. (Malacrea and Vassalli, 1990)

Some very interesting data about the "perception"of the phenomenon (which, in our opinion is the main issue) come from valuable research about social workers' perceptions of child maltreatment in their area (Campanini and Luppi 1993). Social workers believe that the most common form of abuse is psychological; that different forms of maltreatment are occuring with an "average" incidence in their area, that the incidence of incorrect or ungrounded reports of maltreatment and abuse by neighbours or relatives of the children is high. Fathers are believed to be more often responsible for the abuse; social workers tend to identify with the suffering child or sometimes with the mother even if she is "responsible" for maltreatment.

The roughness of these data is surely an index of how absent in Italy is the sensitivity to child maltreatment and abuse prevailing in many other European countries. While more able and willing to detect forms of social maltreatment and exploitation in juvenile employment or delinquency, Italian researchers still hesitate in front of the door of the family home or of traditional caring places, like schools or institutes. The above cited familistic ideology represents an obstacle in understanding. An indirect index of the modest extent of discussion about child abuse may be seen by checking bibliographies: a very complete and up-to-date text about intrafamilial child abuse (Malacrea and Vassalli, 1990) presents over 362 bibliographic entries but only 47 Italian titles.

Child abuse is a particular zone of childhood suffering to which professional social workers gained sensitivity only at the end of the '80s.
Those who, from '70 to '80, examined the phenomenon, were prone to intervene and interpret its causes in sociological terms.
Disease, in its different forms from madness to addiction, in our scientific tradition is mostly considered as social disease. Let us consider the interpretation of mental health problems mirrored by the law suppressing mental health hospitals (n. 180, 1978): it explained and treated the problem chiefly as a social one. Let us consider the same organization of our social services which are, as we will see, centred territorially as a social, political, geographical unit.

But some leading projects, like the centre for the maltreated child in Milano, C.B.M., founded in 1984, are developing a new and different interpretation and treatment. Let us quote the interpretation of intrafamilial sexual abuse developed by the Centre: " Incest between father and daughter .... can happen because a series of psychopathological changes of family structure have happened... which go from children's "parentification", or to rendering one of the parents like a child or as someone excluded, to the seductive activation of one of the children, creating a total role confusion. The whole familial group is somehow part of this confused overturning and contributes to leaving it a secret." (Saraval, 1990, XII. our translation). The philosophy of C.B.M. intervention, in the words of one of its workers, Cirillo, is : "behind a maltreated child there is a suffering family". This trend clearly is opposite to an exclusively repressive answer to the problem of abuse, an answer which has been too often given (Pomodoro 1984). In fact compulsory therapies are used by the C.B.M. centre.

Mass media messages about dramatic cases which now more and more emerge are mostly depicted in terms of sociological explanations, that is overcrowding, misery, unemployment. When this interpretation is not viable madness is often invoked. Children as witnesses are considered to be doubtful by public opinion although courts accept their evidence, even videotaped during an interview with their therapist. Mass media seek to ignore the strange phenomenon of the increasing number of cases discovered, which is in fact closely connected to the more widespread sensitivity of teachers and social workers. Moreover, social workers are often considered to be people who steal children; the title of an intriguing book about social workers, criticizing mass media opinion is actually entitled *"L'assistente sociale ruba i bambini?"* (Cirillo S., Cipolloni M.V., 1994, *"Do social workers steal children?"*). When social workers intervene removing the child from a miserable environment they are often accused of unfairness to poor people. Interventions are often criticized, more than the lack of them.

The legal context

We decided to begin examining the legal context, that is laws and welfare agencies for children, from the fascist period, 1922-1943. During this period, in fact, many welfare laws were promulgated, often completely changing the previous regulative settlement. Italy had become a unitary country quite a short time before, great industrial transformations had just started. Consequently very few laws addressed the protection of individuals in general terms and even less children's rights. We can find only some regulations about working hours for children.

In the story of Italian laws the fascist period is important because great care was given to the reform of social security and welfare. National boards were founded creating security and "specific" welfare systems, intended for every category.

Categorizing persons under the welfare scheme was a tendency which lasted until the law of reform of 1975 which reunified their care attributing them to the municipality.

During the fascist period the following child care boards were founded:

- National Board for helping motherhood and infancy (O.N.M.I.) for infancy and youth care
- Board for helping war orphans (O.N.O.G.)
- Board for helping worker's orphans (E.N.A.O.L.I.)
- Provinces were authorised to help illegitimate children; the "wording" of illegitimate children lasted in Italian laws until 1975 when the family law was reformed.

Current laws assure basic children's rights primarily in the same Italian Constitution (1948 - articles 29, 30, 31) which presents the natural family as the core site for personality development and as the site of choice for satisfying children's rights. This point of view was aimed at countering the strong tendency to receive poor family children into institutions, very often ruled by religious orders.

These articles, accepting the most advanced psychosocial trends for that time, were the grounding norm for the process of de-institutionalization during the seventies. The Italian Constitution states some other childrens' rights like the one relating to the full development of one's own personality, to education (art. 30), to salary equity and to health (arts. 3, 34, 37, 32). "The Duty and right of the parents is to support, to educate and train the children, also those who were born outside the marriage. Where the parents are not capable the law provides for these tasks." It is noteworthy that in a catholic country children of "irregular" families explicitly had the same rights as those of regular families.

Duties and inabilities of parents regarding children are very vaguely defined not only in the Constitution Bill, but in the civil code too. The law states only the rule, without discussing what is meant as duties or inabilities of the parents concerning children (arts. 330, 343, 400 and fls., 433 and fls.). Art. 33 describes parent's behaviour harmful to children: "When one or both parents' behavior is not such as to allow the loss of parental authority certified by art.330, but still looks to be detrimental to the child, the judge (arts. 38,51) can adopt appropriate proceedings to the circumstances and can even state the removal of the child from home."

Since the official publication of the Italian Constitution in 1948 the children's interest in law appears only with act n.431 for children's adoption on June 5, 1967. This is the first of a series of acts pertaining to minors during the golden seventies (as these years are defined by Saraceno 1990 in relation to child care). We will now follow the history of acts relating to children.

a) On December 1, 1970, act n. 898, about divorce, states, among other matters, that "the judge who pronounces sentence of divorce must take every measure for the sake of the minor childrens' interest when their parents divorce or part."

b) On May 19, 1975, reforming family law, in the act n.152, the right of the child to the defence of his moral and material interests is stated again and states that paternal authority will be exerted by both parents and no longer only by the father.

c) Act 194 of 1978 states that minors can use health services, when 14 years old, without their parents' permission; in particular that girls are allowed to interrupt their pregnancy without their parents being informed.

d) Act 405 of 1975 instituted advisory bureaux for the family to promote responsible fatherhood and motherhood; from then on advisory bureaux were strongly health oriented. As years went by, they became out patients' departments.

e) In 1977 by a decree of the President of the Republic, n. 616, the Government committed to local authorities the protection of children. Many very meaningful trends can be found in this decree, like for instance the obligation to watch over the psycho-social state of children and the obligation to found services for the protection of children.
In this same decree, all the national welfare boards in defence of specific categories of people (like workers' orphans or illegitimate children, etc.) founded during the fascist period were abolished.

f) In 1978, act n. 833 founded the national health service, abolishing all the other health boards and declared every citizens' right to health welfare. Every child had to have a paediatrician taking care of him.

g) Shortly after, 1983, act n. 184 regulated adoptions and foster placements widening and reforming the above mentioned law about adoption. Foster placements, statutory as well as by agreement of the parties were for the first time wholly placed on a legal foundation.
There is no precise reference in this act to abuse or maltreatment: specific reasons for adoption or foster placement still make reference to the "inadequate family". The concept of a child's right to live in his natural family is stated again; and only when this family looks to be temporarily incapacitated, can foster placement be started.

(h) Only in the recent act n. 66, 15.2.96, against sexual abuse and rape, are these two crimes considered as crimes against the person and no longer against morals. Until recently, in fact, as crimes against morals, these crimes would be prosecuted only by someone's complaint and not "ex officio". This same law defines rape against a child as an aggravating circumstance.

The civil code, in relation to children's defence defines a concept of defence with a legal more than a welfare meaning and as children's right to be helped at different stages of their life. A legal representative for the child is in fact allowed to commit the child he is taking care of to an institution. This concept of defence is therefore clearly intended for orphan minors and almost exclusively for administering the minors' estate. Laws pertaining to minors are extremely scattered.

Child care agencies and institutions
The institutions involved in child protection are the following:

(a) Ordinary courts in defence of minors when adjudicating about separation and divorce.

(b) Juvenile court, in every child care case, apart from those subject to the ordinary court. This latter has a social service bureau of its own.

(c) The municipality involved in developing services for every child and having specific responsibility for the protection of children needing help. The municipality intervenes in cooperation with the juvenile court which has the power to impose child protecting measures. Most of the social workers are employed by the municipality.

(d) Tutelary judge for every child not having any juridical defence.

The municipal authority has to watch over all the minor citizens living in its area. Almost every Italian municipality (there are about 8100) has enrolled or will in a short time enroll, a full time or part time social worker.

Citizens of every municipality can also access the services of the health authority like infant neuropsychiatry and rehabilitation services for under 16 years olds. Municipalities, social units and the largest and better organized town schools too, are going to enter into agreements of cooperation where currently there is no specific reference to the problem of neglect or abuse. Therefore the responsibility of child protection will still remain with local authorities.

Private boards in agreement with public authorities provide placements for children. Institutions are almost wholly organized by religious boards even if increasingly using lay personnel. Unfortunately institutions too often work without being connected to the social work services of the municipality. They mostly offer a function of relief without providing projects for the psychological and affective development of the children.

The few lay institutions have often changed into little communities. They operate in cooperation with the social work services of the municipality and the juvenile court, mostly offering a first aid placement which would not be easily feasible in a familial setting. They are quite widespread, about 50 in a region like Lombardia. The above mentioned Istituto degli Innocenti, for instance, hosts nowadays a children's home and a mother and child home for recently delivered children. In this foundation children will live just a few weeks.

A quite recent phenomenon are family homes ("case-famiglia") or families who act as foster families. They generally follow a Catholic stand and are connected to voluntary organizations. Deeply different from religious institutions, they have a familial structure and they accept help in terms of everyday living from volunteers. Family-homes are precious resources for children and for social workers; there remain some problems in their relationship with the services for different administrative and methodological reasons.

Voluntary work without any religious background is less frequent but growing in recent years. This kind of voluntary work is characterized by associations treating some specific issue like foster placement and, quite often, violence to women and children. Blue Telephone ("Telefono Azzurro") must be mentioned as a free charge telephone line for children experiencing whatever difficulty. The association has its head office in Bologna, but receives calls and is well known all over the country.

Women's associations against violence are quite widespread at a local level. These associations rarely offer more than consulting services, and not placements, but the trend is to develop these services.

As to organization and collaboration between services: law 194 of 1977 (founding consultancy bureaux for mothers and children) aimed to gather together all the sources of helping interventions in defence of minors. After a short initial period of cooperation these bureaux developed, as we stressed before, a policy of mainly medical intervention, mostly neglecting to cooperate with other socio-psychological workers.

Some comments about laws and child care agencies

Currently acts are scattered, and present laws which accumulated over time, often show contrasting trends.

There is no unitary corpus enunciating the core principles of children's rights. Nor is there any law stating specific services and welfare interventions to be applied in child protection. This failure can be seen as a serious lack of direction and interest in this domain. The law-makers have only enunciated principles without ever identifying specific issues. This has left much room for interpretation by every worker in the psycho-social as well as juridical domain.

Difficulties in the relationship and collaboration between municipality and juvenile courts are now very frequent.

It has moreover to be stressed that national acts in this domain have been for many years only framework-laws. Every region has issued markedly different acts operationalising them. This fact, together with other reasons, creates great differences in service organization and in interventions for children and their families across the whole country. As a consequence of the local interpretations of national laws, proceedings vary between the different regions. Proceedings confirm the local prevailing tradition. This phenomenon can be seen in the provision for recovering children needing care in institutions even though the law considers a familial environment as being preferable for children. This provision is more widespread in the South of Italy, where institutions are more frequent. On the other hand institutions can survive where the social workers "send" new clients to them.

Let us review the reasons for great differences among social workers in different regions:

(a) there is no legal clarity. Every worker has to decide the act which can be applied in a legal context which is very complex and often difficult to interprete.

(b) Services are organized in different ways. This means that some municipal authorities do not excercise responsibility for child protection, awarding it to the national health service.

(c) There is no national observatory for child care.

(d) There are no common training projects for social workers.

This means, for instance, that in Milano there is a private and specific centre for maltreated and abused children and their families, which operates by agreement with the Municipality of Milano, and collaborates with the university as well as the minors's department in the police headquarters. In Firenze the department of minors has just been recently placed in the police headquarters while the municipal authority is directly responsible only for the foster placement service; in Palermo there is no department or centre at all to whom social workers and families can turn.

As law stands, the problem of child abuse and maltreatement is not tackled, at least in many parts of the country, by an autonomous organization of services able to provide specific professional knowledge and interventions.

While the law entitles the municipal authority to address child protection, we have already mentioned the differences among the regions in operationalising the law. A common phenomenon is that while there are enough social workers for the various child problems like disability, mental health, social marginalisation or neglect, there are very few social workers who have to take care of abused children. This problem, not yet clearly perceived, is specific to social workers as they are the only ones who can intervene without the users' consent. On the contrary Italian services stereotypically require the users' consent, to allow services to intervene. Even psychiatrists have not yet developed methods and intervention strategies for people who do not want help. Social workers are requested to intervene in these cases, but their methods and instruments for intervening are still lacking.

As things are, it happens quite often that the teacher, the psychologist or the family physician report their suspicion of abuse to the social worker so as to delegate the responsibility for intervention out of a misguided sense of privacy. Only the emergency ward of the hospitals will immediately report suspicions of abuse to the legal authority. The difficult task is often to go on from the suspicion, even when well grounded, to a report to the Juvenile court and then intervention.

In law and in present tradition there are modest signs of a new, developing tendency, towards citizens' or users' empowerment. For instance 14 year old children can be heard when the judge is deciding about their future, for example in divorce cases.

More relevant to the domain of sociological research is the criticism of socialisation as a potentially abusing process. Socializing agencies ought to develop an approach more sensitive to the actual world and needs of the child (Donati 1980).

Italian laws are chiefly aimed at "protecting" children. If (as the English jurist King (1982) sets out the issue of welfare policy for minors) there are "kiddy-libbers" and "child-savers", we are still at the beginning of a complete "saving" policy. Maybe these points of view represent two progressive steps forward.

Moreover, nothing is happening in relation to parents: there are not yet self help groups for maltreating parents; nor organized groups which can help (or challenge) the social workers' interventions.

Present problems

We will try to focus on problems pertaining to social worker intervention rather than the state of childhood in general, which we have already addressed.

Sensitivity to child maltreatment is certainly well established among social workers, but not so much in relation to child sexual abuse: following Vassalli (1990) we are at the "first stages". The phenomenon is surely underestimated by social workers who are not fully aware of the specific signs nor really able to "see" them. At the same time, a considerable portion (97%) of social workers, according to research by Ventimiglia (1993), believe that different kinds of abuse are still unknown to services as well as to the courts.

Consequently those people who, though closer to children, are not specifically trained to detect it, like teachers or paediatricians, are even more unaware of abuse problems. The scarcity of reporting by schools has been emphasised (Pomodoro 1984). Gyneacologists are generally involved in cases of suspicion of female abuse, but their ability in reporting as experts is considered to be faulty (Maggioni, 1990).

In understanding the point of view of social workers (Campanini 1993), their own problem is the emotional impact of treating child maltreatment, increased by their professional isolation. In fact the social worker has to largely deal alone with the first stage of the case. The interventions of the other helping institutions, like those by the health services or by the Juvenile or penal judge may be ineffective because they are not coordinated, following different time schedules. Italian courts work very slowly, an average penal judgement takes about 2 years.

The social worker often tries to postpone a formal report, thinking she/he can best manage the case in this way. The law does not leave any discretionary power of this kind even when there are simply suspicions of maltreatment or abuse. In this situation the intervention by the judge is used as a last resort in the work with the family.

The rules to be followed, for intervention and treatment, once the crime has been reported are never clear. Every social worker has somehow to create a way of intervening of their own. This can be creative, but unfair for the clients. For instance, while foster families are quite easily available for placement when removing maltreated children from home, standards for choosing these families are lacking. It has happened that foster families have also turned out to be maltreating and abusing.

Future developments
Let us foresee some trends in the future for child care in Italy.
Two appalling dangers are menacing child care.
In the down-swing of economic resources, private as well as public, with an unemployment rate around 10% and harsh financial plans, social welfare funds will be more and more in demand, more and more curtailed. The Government, the Parliament and citizens also believe that welfare funds have to be better used as, in the past, there was certainly a waste of public money. This is not easily achieved: the whole country and local organization need to be reformed; there is no law reorganizing social welfare.

Another danger is represented by the now growing number of children migrating to our country, leaving their own countries where their survival is impossible. We have already referred to the outdated crimes of holding Albanian children under duress.

Apart from these very visible problems, as child care is such a culturally ruled domain, misunderstandings will develop between the services and families of different cultures and ethnic groups in this first period of interethnic contact.

The social network of solidarity still holds an important role even when struggling with problems of organization and lack of time. This is particularly true for small towns which still form the great part of Italy. Even so, this network, which holds the social tissue together, works best for Italian citizens. Apart from a few organizations, this network marginalizes people like those belonging to the Rom, the Chinese or the Moroccan community.

The currently developing ability in detecting abuse and maltreatment ought to be carried further. Specific training programs ought to involve not only social workers, but psychiatrists, paediatricians and teachers; a great effort in this direction is being developed, mostly by feminist groups.

Another new, growing form of intervention is the foundation of family mediation services. These services are urgently needed in facilitating parents' separation.

The future of child care clearly depends on economic trends and consequently on the funds for welfare, as well as on how the problem of extremely marginalized sections of the population will be solved.
The present danger is the tendency to solve emergency problems and not to develop long-term projects. The State looks to be unable to synergize public and private resources and this produces parallel streams of intervention, fighting each other.

References

Ariès, P., "L'enfant et la vie familiale sous l'ancien régime", Plon, 1960.

Becchi, E., "Umanesimo e Rinascimento" in Becchi, E. and Julia, D.(eds.), "Storia dell'infanzia. Dall'antichità al Seicento", Laterza, 1996.

Burgoni, M., Calanchi, M.G., Magri, O. and Pedrazzoli, G., "Gli indicatori del maltrattamento ai minori e i loro significati" in Campanini , A. (ed.) "Maltrattamento all'infanzia", Nuova Italia Scientifica, 1990.

Campanini, A., "L'assistente sociale e il maltrattamento infantile: appunti a margine di una ricerca", "Rassegna di servizio sociale", XXXII, n.3, 1993.

Campanini, A. (ed.) "Maltrattamento all'infanzia", Nuova Italia Scientifica, 1993.

Campanini, A., and Luppi, F., "L'assistente sociale e il maltrattamento infantile: una ricerca" in Campanini, A. (ed.) "Maltrattamento all'infanzia", Nuova Italia Scientifica, 1993.

Cirillo, S. and Cipolloni, M.V., "L'assistente sociale ruba i bambini?", Cortina, 1994.

Conseil d'Europe, "Comportements et attitudes sexuelles et leur implications sur le droit pénal", Comité européen pour les problèmes criminels, Strasbourg, 1984.

Cornia, G.,"Distribuzione del reddito ed equità intergenerazionale", in Ministero dell'Interno. Direzione Generale dei Servizi Civili (ed.), "Politiche sociali per l'infanzia e l'adolescenza", Unicopli, 1991.

Corrado, S., "Alcune considerazioni sugli indici in campo scolastico" in "Scuola Democratica", XII, January-June, 1989.

Donati, P., "Equità generazionale e nuova cittadinanza", in
Ministero dell'Interno. Direzione Generale dei Servizi Civili (ed.), "Politiche sociali per l'infanzia e l'adolescenza", Unicopli, 1991.

Donati, P., "Socializzazione o abuso all'infanzia? Contraddizioni e dilemmi in prospettiva sociologica" in Caffo, E. (ed.), "Abusi e violenza all'infanzia", Unicopli, 1980.

King, 1982, quoted by Théry, I. "La convenzione dell'O.N.U. sui diritti del bambino, nascita di una nuova ideologia" in Ministero dell'Interno. Direzione Generale dei Servizi Civili (ed.) "Politiche sociali per l'infanzia e l'adolescenza", Unicopli, 1991.

L.A.B.O.S., 1984-87 (ed.), quoted by Viggiani, L. and Tressanti, S.," Violenza ai minori in Italia", "Esperienze di Giustizia minorile", n.3-4, 1991.

Maggioni, C., "Il ruolo del medico" in Malacrea, M., Vassalli. A. (eds.) "Segreti di famiglia", Cortina, Milano, 1990.

Malacrea, M., Vassalli, A. (eds.), "Segreti di famiglia. L'intervento nei casi di incesto", Cortina, 1990.

Pombeni, M.L.: "L'adolescente e la scuola", in Palmonari, A. (ed.) "Psicologia dell'adolescenza", Il Mulino, 1993.

Pomodoro, L., "Problemi giuridici delle violenze sessuali ai minori" in "La violenza nascosta", Cortina, 1984.

Rapporto sulla condizione dell'Infanzia in Italia, Ministero degli affari sociali (ed.), 1996.

Saraceno, C.: "Povertà e condizione dei minori in Italia dagli anni Cinquanta ad oggi", Unicef, Istituto degli Innocenti, 1990.

Saraval, A.: Foreword to "Segreti di famiglia", Malacrea, M. and Vassalli, A. (eds.) "Segreti di famiglia. L'intervento nei casi di incesto", Cortina, 1990.

Shamgar-Handelman, L.,:"Infanzia e giustizia distributiva" in Ministero dell'Interno. Direzione Generale dei Servizi civili (ed.), "Politiche sociali per l'infanzia e l'adolescenza", Unicopli, 1991.

Spini, V.,: "Introduzione ai lavori del seminario internazionale sui problemi dei minori", in Ministero dell'Interno. Direzione Generale dei Servizi civili (ed.), "Politiche sociali per l'infanzia e l'adolescenza", Unicopli, 1991.

Vassalli, A., "L'abuso sessuale sui bambini, definizione, caratteristiche e conseguenze", in Malacrea, M. and Vassalli, A. (eds.), "Segreti di famiglia. L'intervento nei casi di incesto", Cortina, 1990.

Ventimiglia C.,: "La differenza negata. Ricerca sulla violenza sessuale in Italia", Angeli, 1987.

Ventimiglia, C.: "La violenza sui minori, tra realtà e rappresentazione sociale" in Cambi, F. and Ulivieri, S. :"Infanzia e violenza. Forme, terapie, interpretazioni", La Nuova Italia, 1990.

Ventimiglia, C.: "Infanzia e rappresentazione sociale" in Campanini, A. (ed.) "Maltrattamento all'infanzia", Nuova Italia Scientifica, 1993.

Conclusion:
Transnational Comparisons and Future Trajectories

By Keith Pringle and Margit Harder

If at the end of the twentieth century there is some growing realisation that child abuse constitutes a pressing social problem across the countries of Europe, then what are the commonalities of experience among those countries? And what scope is there for cooperation and mutual learning in challenging this social problem? In this volume, the contributors have surveyed past, current and future trends in five European countries. Here in the concluding chapter we present our own personal overview of that material, tease out transnational commonalities/divergences and attempt to sketch future trends as we enter the new millennium.

The introductory chapter to this comparative study drew attention to some of the inadequacies of previous attempts to provide transnational analyses of social welfare systems generally. In that connection, this study attempts to fill part of the gap in previous transnational analyses, whilst also recognising the close in-ter-relationship between age, gender, "race", sexuality, class and disability as dimensions of social disadvantage in the lived experience of welfare service users.

Before offering our analysis, we need to offer one important caveat. As we also slightly touched upon in the Introduction, transnational comparison of welfare services which are largely non-quantifiable is fraught with problems. Not the least of these is the fact that such services vary in their format from one country to another (Lorenz 1994, Munday and Ely 1996, Pringle 1997). As we have seen and as we shall see, this certainly applies to child protective services across Europe. But more broadly it also applies to the general concept of "social services". Let us offer one of the most straightforward examples of this diversity: in many European states such as Denmark, Italy and Finland, provision of financial resources is a major part of the remit for some social worker posts. In England and Wales and in the Republic of Ireland, cash benefit allocation is not the direct responsibility of social workers. In the analysis which follows we must constantly bear in mind that social work itself, and not simply child protection, is a function of the past and present cultural/social/economic/political milieux found in different countries - and indeed can sometimes vary between the regions of a single country.

The various essays in this study reveal a highly complex transnational picture of convergence and divergence in protective services. It seems logical to begin our illustration of this by considering patterns of historical development of protective services for children.

Historical development of child protective services

The national essays by Buckley, Harder and Pringle reveal a degree of overlap regarding the important developments which took place in Ireland, Denmark and England at the end of the nineteenth century, culminating in each case with a piece of relatively specific child protective legislation at that time or in the first decade of the century which followed. We should note that the symmetry between Ireland and England is easily understandable given that the former was ruled at that time by the latter.

Despite their Nordic cultural commonalities, Finland and Denmark followed rather different trajectories at this period, no doubt partly due to the particular political circumstances of Finland emphasised by Tuomista and Vuori-Karvia in their essay: subjection to Sweden, then to Russia and finally civil war.

As for Italy, Bini and Toselli reveal that a strong continuity of themes characterises the picture there from the Renaissance right down to the present day: local variability in perceptions of child maltreatment and limitations placed upon such perceptions by the relative scarcity of public resources and the extensive ideological and cultural influence of the Roman Catholic Church. A comparable influence has, of course, often been attributed to that Church in Ireland, with good reason as Buckley notes. However, the political unity with the United Kingdom imposed on Ireland seems to have been a more critical factor at this period in determining the structure of responses to child maltreatment.

From the early twentieth century onwards, there is no simple all-embracing pattern to the developments which occurred. However, at least one element seems common to most of the countries in our study. For the development of child protective services in almost all of them represents an oscillation between approaches to families which we might characterise as punitive/judicial on the one hand and welfare-oriented on the other. Moreover, we shall see that these oscillations have often been reflected in legislative changes. We now address this process of oscillation.

Such oscillations were already apparent in late nineteenth century Ireland and England. In the latter, they continued with welfare-oriented laws of the 1960s subsequently being replaced with more punitive approaches in the 1970s and 1980s. In the present day, as Pringle stresses, current debates about Child Protection versus Family Support within the ambiguous legislative frame of the Children Act 1989 maintain the picture of oscillation.

In Ireland, a period of legislative fixity occurred from 1908 until 1991 but the punishment-welfare debate continued and remains current. Buckley's analysis suggests that this debate, in the period since independence, has been influenced at different times by numerous variables. Not the least of these has been the conception of the family promulgated by the Catholic Church and thereby enshrined within the Republic's Constitution. Another important variable in more recent decades has been the professional aspirations of such categories of welfare personnel as social workers and paediatricians, a point also highlighted by Pringle in relation to England.

Furthermore, post-war debates in the Republic appear to have been heavily influenced by experiences across the sea in England, not least the strong trend in the 1980s towards a Child Protection model. This English model is characterised by a relatively punitive, targeted response and the virtual elimination of preventive and therapeutic services in favour of child abuse investigations. However, the English influence has been mediated by other important factors specific to Ireland including the historic role of the Catholic Church regarding both family ideology and service provision and the long-standing scarcity of public welfare resources. As we shall see, these are factors which have had a similar, but at the same time different, impact in Italy. In Ireland a specifically Irish pattern of service response seems to be developing as these factors interact with public "scandals" associated with intra-familial and extra-familial child abuse. And both forms of scandal seem to be striking at the heart of some national assumptions and practices there.

In Denmark, Harder traces the complex oscillation of punishment/judicial and welfare orientations which also continues into the present. In some respects there appear to be considerable similarities between Denmark and England in terms of recent variables even if these have operated with different timescales. In both countries, financial restrictions on a hitherto relatively generous welfare structure have been/are an important factor and so too is the switch-over of welfare support and punitive response in work with families which may occur from one day to another and which creates such role tension for many social workers.

However, once again the historical perspective discloses complexity and challenges a simplistic categorisation of countries. For despite what has been said, the present pattern of services in Denmark still presents a very different profile from that to be found in England and Wales. In the latter country, as we have seen, prevention and therapy are almost absent in child care social work and the current balance in the punishment/judicial versus welfare debate is heavily skewed towards the former (even if the British government is now seeking to alter this). There may be some pressures pushing Denmark in the direction of England. However, the evidence from our survey suggests that Denmark still has a long way to go before it replicates the English situation and that this is hardly likely to happen in either the short or longer-term.

Despite its very different historical trajectory, in some ways the development of services in Finland over the decades since the Second World War provides closer parallels with Denmark. Once again this development has been characterised by tensions between punishment/judicial and welfare perspectives, the 1983 Act setting a far more welfare-oriented agenda than the 1937 law, as Tuomisto and Vuori-Karvia point out. The present state of the debate in Finland is far more oriented towards welfare than punishment/judicial, and thereby considerably closer to the situation in Denmark than that in either Ireland or England. To a large extent services in both Denmark and Finland for child maltreatment are subsumed within a much broader range of services to promote the positive welfare of all children. Such a state of affairs is virtually unthinkable in England where it would be fairer to say that services to promote the welfare of children have been displaced by an almost exclusive focus on child abuse (Cannan 1992, Pringle 1995). In fact, our study suggests that out of all five countries, Finland is in practice more aligned to a welfare approach than any other nation including Denmark. However, as the

Finnish chapter also underlines, a current and conspicuous change in social values is taking place. The 1993 change in the Finnish system towards increasing the independence and jurisdiction of local authorities might add to this change in social values.

As for Italy, Bini and Toselli suggest that post-war development of child maltreatment services remains very limited in general terms, and locally variable in specific ones. We have already alluded to some of the reasons for this situation including the ideological influence of Roman Catholicism, the traditionally minimal role of the state in welfare provision, and a relative lack of welfare resources particularly in the South (Ferrara 1996, Spano 1996). Other issues relevant to this situation of variability and low level provision may be the marked decentralisation of social service provision in Italy and the lack of widespread feminist perspectives there especially compared to England. We shall discuss this latter point at more length later in the chapter.

Some of the continuities and discontinutities between the different welfare systems in relation to child maltreatment can also be further gauged by examining the way child abuse has been conceptualised over time in the different countries. And it is to this that we now turn.

Definitions of child abuse

Perhaps not surprisingly, a review of the way child abuse has been defined over time and across welfare systems discloses patterns not dissimilar to those we identified above regarding historical development of welfare responses. There is now general agreement that child abuse should be regarded as a social construction, at least to some extent (Hallett 1995). Consequently, an examination of the process of social construction over time may be a useful way of "excavating" the assumptions which a society makes about the phenomenon of child abuse. The material in our study allows us to undertake such excavation in relation to the five countries in question.

It is clear from the chapter by Bini and Toselli that in present-day Italy relatively little attention is still given to the issue of child abuse either in terms of public opinion or professional concern compared to the other countries. As a result, it should not surprise us that the constitution of child abuse remains largely unaddressed in terms of research and more generally. This is illustrated by the way that Bini and Toselli, with great creativity, draw upon a wide range of relatively indirect source materials to explore the idea of child abuse. What is particularly striking when we compare this with the situation in other countries is the very low current profile accorded to the subject of sexual abuse in Italian professional and public circles. We can speculate about the reasons for this. Several commentators (Armstrong and Hollows 1991, Pringle 1993, 1997) have suggested that issues such as the extent to which a society recognises the autonomous social rights of children and the degree to which feminist perspectives have a radical voice within a society may often be crucial factors. The ideological force of the Church and the deeply familial focus of Italian society can militate against both of them.

Once again, however, we must guard ourselves against oversimplification on several counts. First, as Bini and Toselli make abundantly clear, it is never wise to construct sweeping statements about a country so regionally diverse as Italy. In particular, we must register the fact that perceptions often differ between urban and rural areas, between regions and, perhaps most crucially, between regions of the North, Centre and South. Thus Bini and Toselli describe some professional initiatives, especially in Milano, which address a wide range of abusive behaviours, including sexual abuse, using a family systems approach. They also make reference to the work of "Case delle Donne" which frequently focus on abusive behaviour towards women and children from a feminist perspective - and these, too, are far more common in North and Central Italy.

A second reason for caution about overgeneralising is that much of what we have said about the ideological predominance of the Church and deep familialism is also true of Ireland and yet the current definition about the problem there differs considerably from that in Italy. This is not to say that Church and familial ideology have been/are unimportant for Ireland. Buckley makes very clear that such factors have played a crucial role over the years in limiting the extent to which child abuse has been defined and addressed especially in the public arena. Yet the fact remains that not only is child abuse, indeed sexual abuse, one of the most high profile current social issues in Ireland but that professional attention towards child abuse has relatively deep historical roots. As Buckley points out, in 1975 the Irish Department of Health had already set up a committee on "non-accidental injury" (NAI) to children and the first professional guidance was published as early as

1977. Clearly the process by which child abuse has now been socially constructed in Ireland differs markedly from that in Italy, despite cultural similarities which are not always superficial. Why should this be?

Part of the reason surely lies in some of the historical factors alluded to earlier in this chapter. Buckley notes that in the 1960s and 1970s the ISPCC played a central role in disseminating U.S. and U.K. material on NAI within Ireland: in other words the professional structures initiated at the end of the nineteenth century in Ireland, parallel to those created in North America and Britain, were of importance. So too, probably, is the more general cultural proximity which links Ireland to the U.S. and the U.K., including in both cases the issue of language.

When we turn to England and Wales in relation to the social construction process, we once again find a picture which parallels and connects with our earlier summary of historical developments. In both cases, the situation in England and Wales represents the polar opposite to that which pertains to Italy. In the former country, specific state definitions of child abuse and maltreatment have been of central concern both professionally and publically since at least the end of the nineteenth century. The overall trend has been parallel to that in the United States: a steady inflation in definitions of what constitutes child abuse (Stevenson 1989). Unlike Italy but similar to the U.S., in England over the last decade the issue of sexual abuse has become highly prominent professionally and publically.

To some extent the explanation of these phenomena in England and Wales are readily understandable in terms of the factors we have already addressed in relation to Italy and Ireland. For in the United Kingdom, the ideological hold of the Church has been far weaker than in the other two countries especially in this century. At the same time a very strong women's movement has developed in Britain in the years since the second world war and radical feminist perspectives have been important in this process, though not exclusively so (Kelly 1988, Jeffreys 1990, Segal 1990). Thus some potential sources of resistance to state intervention in family life have been relatively absent in England and Wales whilst other forces have positively impelled social encouragement of broader definitions of child abuse, and this particularly relates to sexual abuse.

However, as usual, the picture is not so simple as we might like to believe. For there are other features of British society which do not correspond with the relatively broad definitions of child abuse which have now developed there nor with the state interventionist machine represented by the English model of Child Protection discussed by Pringle. After all the United Kingdom, which lacks both a written Constitution and a Bill of Rights, is by no means a european leader in enshrining the rights of children in law (see Ruxton 1996 for detailed european comparisons). Moreover, as Pringle makes clear in this study, England is characterised by strong familial ideologies of a patriarchal nature despite the lack of a Roman Catholic ethic. In such a context how are we to explain the profound family interventionism of the English Child Protection model?

To a large extent the explanation lies in the precise form of that interventionism. In comparing British and French methods of child protection Cooper et al. (1995) make the point that the French approach probably entails more frequent interventions but these are often less punitive and more supportive than the British approach. In other words what marks out British family interventionism regarding child abuse is not so much its extent but its particularly punitive nature.

Cooper et al. (1995) relate these phenomena to the different cultural perspectives in the two countries relating this to the concept of social solidarity. In France an intimate and mutually supportive connection is assumed between the well-being of "society" and the well-being of its basic unit, "the family" - and this approach is linked to France's Catholic heritage and revolutionary history. Such an optimistic perspective both sanctions relatively frequent involvement of public (or publically-funded) professionals in family life and the generally supportive and welfare-oriented nature of that involvement. By contrast, Cooper et al. (1995) characterise England as adopting a far more individualistic, rather than solidaristic, approach to the family. Whereas in France the family is celebrated as being central to the fabric of society, in Britain it is regarded defensively as a bulwark in favour of individual rights (especially the individual rights of men) against what is historically a relatively centralised state power.

Such an analysis based on hegemonic cultural themes fits well with Pringle's depiction of the English Child Protection model. After all, that model's central dynamic is a sharp separation out of a "dangerous" minority of individuals and families from the large majority of the population who are assumed to be "good" people. Thus the English Child Protection model does not threaten the vast majority of "englishmen in their castles".

What is noticeably lacking in this portrait of hegemonic English cultural themes is any sense of social solidarity. Some would argue that this profound absence of social solidarity in much of English cultural life is one of the most crucial factors marking out British welfare approaches from those in states such as France with a Catholic heritage and also (but for different historical reasons) from those in the Nordic countries (Pringle 1997).

In terms of the social construction of child abuse, the situations in Denmark and Finland do seem similar, certainly in comparison with the other three countries surveyed in this volume. What is interesting in this respect about the accounts offered by Harder and by Tuomisto and Vuori-Karvia is the relative extent to which child maltreatment is defined within the context of positive models of child care policy in both countries. Moreover, such a definitional perspective is paralleled in both countries by a practice approach which places provision for maltreated children within much broader services designed to positively promote the well-being of all children.

For the purposes of our analysis here, we intend to define this Nordic approach as an undifferentiated one: i.e. there is relatively little tendency to separate out child abuse as a wholly distinct and different phenomenon from the wider context of child care generally. This approach contrasts with the highly differentiated one in England and Wales where child abuse has almost been reified into a separate entity with virtually no connection to wider concerns about promoting positive child care (Parton and Parton 1989).

While it may be true that in a sense Italian definitions of child maltreatment are also subsumed within a model of positive child care, two factors differentiate the Italian approach from the ones in Denmark and Finland. First, as we have already seen, the degree of professional and public attention devoted in Italy to the issue of child maltreatment has been, and continues to be, far smaller than that in either of the two Nordic countries. Secondly, in terms of levels of provision for child maltreatment the gap between Denmark and Finland on the one hand and Italy on the other could hardly be greater.

A different but equally sharp definitional divide also separates these Nordic states from Ireland and England and Wales. It is true that a process of definitional inflation regarding child abuse has occurred over time in Finland and Denmark, which is comparable to the process in England and Wales and Ireland. However, as we have already noted, the dominant current focus in England and Wales is one where child maltreatment is socially constructed and addressed with scant attention to what might be regarded as positive child care: child abuse has in fact virtually displaced child care as the main objective of social welfare practice in England and Wales. Insofar as Ireland has been influenced by trends in the U.K., the same to some extent applies there. However, as we shall see, other cultural influences offer the hope that Ireland may not necessarily go on to replicate this specifically English negativity.

In saying all this it is once more important not to overgeneralise. In particular, we need to recognise that, despite their real commonalities, Denmark and Finland are two different countries with specific histories and cultural milieux which, of course, impact differentially on the way child abuse is socially constructed. Let us give two examples taken from the material in the preceeding chapters.

First, the account by Tuomisto and Vuori-Karvia underlines the importance attached in Finland to the issue of mothers who are judged to be inadequate parents by virtue of alcohol and/or drug abuse. While such an issue is no doubt of concern in some Danish cases (as in some English or Irish ones), the same prominence is not attached to it in the accounts of the other authors in this volume, including that by Harder - and this may well partly relate to different cultural constructions regarding alcohol and drug use which obtain in different countries.

Secondly, it seems clear from the accounts in this volume that Denmark and Finland are not quite in the same place regarding the social importance attached to sexual abuse. In particular sexual abuse seems to have been higher on professional and public agendas in Denmark to the point where, as in England and Wales, a "backlash" to it has been occurring. On the other hand, differences between Denmark and Finland regarding this issue seem less important when they are both compared with England. For instance, it seems that the predominant theoretical model for explaining sexual abuse in both Denmark and Finland is a family systemic one - an approach which has been largely discredited in England. At the same time far more attention seems to be paid in England to sexual abuse which occurs outside the immediate family (especially in social work settings) than is the case either in Denmark or Finland.

Legislative frameworks

As we have suggested earlier in this chapter, the legislative frameworks which operate in each country not only partly determine forms of practice but are themselves to some extent reflections of cultural values and approaches to provision in those countries. Thus there is a dual reason for a comparative study of legislative frameworks.

As one might expect from what has already been said, the two countries most in contrast in this respect are England and Wales on the one hand and Italy on the other. Practice in the former is firmly and specifically guided by a mass of official material comprised of a consolidated Children's Act together with numerous procedural documents specifically related to child abuse from central and local government agencies but tightly co-ordinated by the former. Pringle defines this centralised mountain of documentation devoted to the single issue of child abuse as one of the hallmarks of the English Child Protection model.

Bini and Toselli vividly describe a very different scenario pertaining to Italy. Here the national legislative framework is constituted by a patchwork of different Acts of varying specificity with massive scope remaining for local legislative and practice interpretation.

The Irish situation is now closer to that in England and Wales than to Italy. However, it is significant that in contrast to England which has experienced a long series of child care acts, there has been a massive gap between the major Irish legal reformulations of 1908 and 1991. Moreover, Buckley underlines that the current legislative and procedural situation in Ireland is by no means simply a reflection of the English scenario. For instance, there are major differences between English procedures regarding the involvement of parents in child abuse enquiries and those which operate in Ireland. She also notes that formal procedural etiquette does not necessarily match practice on the ground in Ireland. Despite similar procedural frameworks in the two countries ensuring different agencies "work together", Buckley indicates that this objective is probably far less frequently achieved in Ireland.

Although the major pieces of child welfare legislation in both Ireland and in England and Wales theoretically frame practice for the protection of children and the positive promotion of good child care, the two chapters in this volume reveal that in reality the former objective overwhelms the latter in each country to varying extents. This is partly a result of resource priorities. However, Pringle makes clear that in England it is also as a result of social, political and media considerations (Parton 1996).

By contrast, in Denmark and Finland current legislative frameworks, using a predominantly supportive welfare approach to families, genuinely envisage child maltreatment being addressed within measures for the general promotion of positive child care. Of course the laws in both countries do make provision for legal control of children being ceded to the state in extremis. However, unlike the Child Protection model in England and Wales, such provision in Denmark and Finland is not regarded as virtually the sum-total of social work child care practice. The predominant social work model in the latter two countries is one which is generally supportive to families. Moreover the chronological path by which legislative frameworks in Denmark and Finland developed from punitive/judicial to largely welfare/supportive seems to have been similar in each country.

Once again, we need to qualify the commonality which our analysis has imposed on Denmark and Finland in relation to legislative frameworks: they are, as we have said before, different countries. For instance, the accounts in this study suggest that recent social work child care practice in Denmark is becoming more targeted. However, once again these differences seem less significant when placed next to the English scenario. After all, Harder's account of Denmark makes considerable reference to preventative work and therapeutic assistance, concepts which have ceased to have much real meaning in English social work child care practice.

Finally, we should note some quite dramatic contrasts in the legislative mechanics by which the protection of children is achieved. For instance, a very sharp difference exists between Denmark, on the one hand, and England and Wales, on the other, in terms of the process by which a child is compulsorily removed from her/his family. In Denmark this sort of removal is decided by a social committee of the local municipality consisting of three municipal politicians plus a judge and a psychologist, as described by Harder in her chapter. In other words this mechanism is not primarily judicial and belongs to the same administrative unit (i.e. the local municipality) which is seeking the child's removal. By contrast, since the 1989 Children Act the procedure in England and Wales by which children enter into the compulsory care of the local authority is wholly centred on court processes completely separate from the local authority which is seeking the child's removal.

Current practice in relation to the protection of children

Italian practice matches very closely what we have said under previous headings. Just as the definitional and legislative situation is unclear and variable, so too are the patterns of actual service provision, according to Bini and Toselli. They indicate that this is partly a function of cultural and resource diversity with the major fault-lines occurring once again between North, Central and South Italy. However, Bini and Toselli also attribute variability in services to the structure of welfare provision in Italy: i.e. massive devolvement of responsibility to localities; and within the localities huge problems of specific co-ordination between the various statutory and charitable agencies. The situation is not apparently assisted by the low financial priority often accorded to child maltreatment issues and the frequent lack of services dedicated to this topic except in very specialised and scarce settings.

Paradoxically, the practice situation in England and Wales is both dissimilar and similar to that in Italy. Structurally, the differences between the two countries could not be greater. In England and Wales relatively massive resources are dedicated to protecting children and the organisations charged with implementing this objective are comparatively well-coordinated. However, several English commentators have suggested that the actual objective of protecting children is often not achieved by this apparently impressive Child Protection model (Pringle 1996, 1997). Consequently, it may often be difficult to know whether the variability of provision offered by Italy or the massive protective machine operating in England and Wales is the less effective in helping children.

Partly as a result of critiques of the Child Protection model, and probably for financial reasons as well, the British government has recently recommended that local authorities should provide services geared more to support families rather than to intervene on a punitive/judicial basis. This change may result in a more positive approach to child maltreatment such as allegedly exists in France (Cooper et al 1995) - and perhaps also in Denmark and Finland.

However, there are several reasons why this scenario is not as encouraging as it might seem and we mention two reasons now. First, truly supportive social work child care policies are expensive as both Denmark and Finland are now keenly aware given their financially staitened circumstances - and it seems unlikely that any British government will be willing to underwrite such massive social spending. On the contrary, there is considerable suspicion that the emphasis on family support espoused by the British government is primarily designed to allow dismantling of the inefficient and costly Child Protection machine without any adequate replacement being provided for it.

The second reason why some English commentators do not welcome a predominantly welfare-oriented family support approach to child maltreatment is that they believe it may be as ineffective as the Child Protection model in protecting children, particularly against sexual abuse (see Pringle, this volume). These then are some of the complex practice debates current in England and Wales.

The current practice issues highlighted by Buckley in her chapter on Ireland are reminiscent of some English debates: in particular the gap which frequently exists between the high aspirations of child protection procedures and the less than impressive realities "on the ground". However, as she also points out, Ireland has not so far developed a massive bureaucratic machine such as characterises English practice. And, given the English experience, one can understand why many in Ireland hope that trend can be avoided there.

In addition Buckley stresses the sexist assumptions which in various ways underpin child protection structures and practice in Ireland. That critique can equally be applied to the English situation and beyond: certainly some of Buckley's arguments in this respect are echoed in Pringle's chapter.

Buckley also highlights issues of culture and "race" by referring to the plight of "travellers" within the Irish child protective system. Fruitful transnational comparisons can indeed be made between her comments and those of Bini and Toselli about the "Rom" in Italy and to some extent about the fate of Albanian children there. In Denmark the limited amount of research carried out suggests that there is no overpreponderance there (yet) of children from immigrant or refugee families among those removed from their families due to child abuse. Elsewhere Pringle (1995) has drawn attention to the disadvantaged position of black families in Britain within the Child Protection machine (Barn 1993). Buckley's chapter reminds us that in assessing welfare services for the protection of children we need to address the way such services interact with all forms of social disadvantage including sexism and racism as well as poverty and ageism (Pringle 1995 chapters 3 and 8).

Current practice in Finland, as we have already noted, possesses several notable characteristics. One of the most striking is the relative lack of service differentiation accorded to child abuse. The latter appears to be addressed within an overall practice objective of providing services which promote all children's positive well-being. Such an approach stands in stark contrast to the Child Protection model of England and Wales where child care social work practice is to a large extent confined to issues of child abuse alone. In a less spectacular way the Finnish model also differs markedly from that apparently developing in Ireland.

Despite the immense cultural divide between them, the lack of service differentiation characteristic of Finland resembles the lack of differentiation which we earlier noted in Italy. Unlike England, neither of them dedicates a mass of services specifically to child abuse. Of course, one would not wish to force this comparison too far: in most other respects there are massive differences between Finnish and Italian practice. Not the least of these differences is the infinitely greater resource provision devoted to public child welfare in Finland than in Italy. Nevertheless, it may be fruitful to spend some time considering why Finnish practice is so different from that in Britain and why, in at least this one respect, there is a closer affinity between Italy and Finland.

Some of the answers to this question can be gauged from the concluding comments of Tuomisto and Vuori-Karvia in their chapter. Looking to the future they speculate that Finnish practice may soon have to change direction if (a) financial pressures take their toll and/or (b) child abuse becomes a more major professional/public concern in Finland.

Let us deal with point (a) first. In his chapter Pringle argues that one of the factors shaping the characteristic English Child Protection model in the 1980s was economic: the drive to target scarce public finances. Herein lies at least part of the reason why Finnish and English approaches to the protection of children have been so different: and, indeed, one does wonder what will happen in the future to the relatively generous Finnish provision given that country's massive financial problems.

However, economic considerations are not enough in themselves to explain the interesting configuration between English, Irish, Finnish and Italian child protective approaches. In fact, this takes us on to the second point made by Tuomisto and Vuori-Karvia: the varying extents to which child abuse is on public and professional agendas in the different countries. The material in this book demonstrates that child abuse is far higher on both agendas in England and Ireland than it is in either Finland or Italy. Earlier in the chapter we attempted to shed light on why there should be such a difference between Ireland and Italy when, in at least some respects, they share common cultural features. Here we now want to focus on the configuration between Finland, Italy and England and Wales. Why has child abuse become so important in the latter country compared with the other two?

This is an immensely complex question to which we can only offer a few tentative answers in the space available here. Some of the explanations will inevitably be very specific to the countries involved. For instance, there were specific historical reasons why at certain times it was useful for some categories of welfare workers in Britain to use child abuse as a vehicle by which they might advance the status of their professions (Cannan 1992): Buckley makes a similar point in relation to Ireland. However, other reasons for this agenda-setting configuration between Finland, Italy and England and Wales are probably more structural in origin and we wish to outline one of the most important of these now.

A major clue to this issue lies in the general literature on comparative european welfare systems produced in recent years (Esping-Andersen 1996, Pringle 1997 chapter 1). Despite the many valid critiques of the work of Esping-Andersen and those who have followed him, certain features of his analysis are useful. One important insight from that analysis is the light which can be shed on the degree to which principles of social solidarity influence the formation of different welfare systems (Spicker 1991).

According to the kinds of categorisation suggested by Esping-Andersen (1990) and Leibfried (1993), Finland's welfare regime pertains most closely to the welfare model labelled as "Social Democratic/Scandinavian" (as indeed does Denmark), Italy's to either the "Conservative Corporatist" or "Latin Rim/Catholic Corporatist" models and Britain's to a combination of models of which the "Neo-Liberal" one is perhaps the most significant (Cochrane and Clarke 1993). According to such classifications, principles of social solidarity are said to be important in the formation of the "Social Democratic", "Conservative Corporatist" and "Latin Rim" regimes, albeit for varying historical and cultural reasons. By contrast, those principles of solidarity are said to be distinctly absent from the "Neo-Liberal" model.

In this chapter we have already demonstrated the way the relative absence of principles of social solidarity in the welfare system of England and Wales helps us to understand the particularly individualistic and negative aspects of state interventionism there in relation to Child Protection. More broadly, the cultural absence of a sense of social solidarity helps to explain the markedly residual nature of Britain's welfare provision compared to many of its neighbours in northern and western Europe.

However, in one respect this lack of a solidaristic perspective in Britain may, paradoxically, have some sort of a positive outcome. One could argue that its very absence in Britain has permitted a greater recognition of, and action against, certain social problems which are more politically unsettling in countries where a sense of positive social solidarity exists. And according to Esping-Andersen most other European Union members do fall in to this latter category.

The sorts of social problems we have in mind are those which sharply reveal deep and extensive power imbalances. Societies associated with neo-liberalism, such as Britain, may be far more open about the extent of their social divisions: indeed some sections within those societies may (unforunately) actually celebrate social divisions as necessary for economic success. Consequently, in such societies as Britain social problems associated with deep disadvantage may be both more obvious and more acknowledged than in societies where there is greater aspiration to the ideals of social inclusion and solidarity.

We could apply this perspective to a number of specific social phenomena: for instance, racism. Despite the undoubted inadequacy of British welfare responses to issues of racism (Ahmad 1990), many commentators point out that compared with other members of the European Union the British response is relatively pro-active and forceful because it has recognised more fully the true extent of the social divisions wrought by racism in that country (Rex 1992, Mitchell and Russell 1994).

In terms of our discussion here, we can seek to apply the same approach to the issue of child abuse. Is one reason for the greater recognition of this issue in Britain (compared to Finland and Italy), the relative absence of solidaristic principles there? Is it more possible in Britain than it is in Finland or Italy to acknowledge the deep social divisions and massive power differentials (age, poverty, gender) revealed by the true extent of child abuse? Are such social divisions less visible, though still equally real, in societies which espouse the idea of social solidarity than in Britain? This is one hypothesis by which we might partly explain the fact that Britain has placed child abuse higher on its social agenda than any other country in Europe.

Of course an alternative hypothesis might be that there is simply less child abuse in countries such as Finland or Italy than there is in Britain. Given the relative lack of research in the first two countries, it is hard to know whether that is true or not. Two pieces of (admittedly inconclusive) evidence relating to the specific issue of sexual abuse suggest that it may well not be true. The first is a review of sexual abuse prevalence surveys across the world carried out by David Finkelhor (1991). He concluded that lower prevalence rates discovered by surveys in some countries (including many in continental Europe) could largely be attributed to the research methodologies which those surveys had adopted. Finkelhor also concluded that on the whole those surveys producing the highest prevalence rates (regardless of location) were the ones which had adopted the most reliable research methodologies.

The second piece of evidence relates to recent events in a number of European countries. As we have noted earlier, Buckley describes the long-standing societal sources of resistance to a full recognition of child abuse (and especially sexual abuse) in Ireland. Only a few years ago, any one suggesting that sexual abuse was a major problem in Ireland would probably have been regarded as eccentric by most people. Such a dismissal now has a very hollow ring in view of the revelations which have occurred there relating to abuse both inside and outside the family circle. Similarly, events in Belgium have shocked the populace there out of their assumption that such occurrences happened only in countries like Britain (for instance see "The European" newspaper, 22-28 August 1996). In addition these revelations have to be taken in the context of a growing awareness regarding the extent of paedophilic sex tourism by West Europeans not only to East Asia but also to the newly "liberated" countries of Eastern Europe ("The European", 30 November-6 December 1996). Men from Germany, France and Scandinavia figure prominently in this trade, as well as British.

To summarise: the relative lack of differentiation in service provision regarding child abuse in Finland does probably reflect in part the much more generous resourcing of child care services there compared to England and Wales where financial stringency has contributed to the sharp focus on child abuse. However, the situation in Finland may also result from the much lower profile accorded to child abuse there at both the public and professional levels. Such a lower profile for child abuse characterises many other West European countries including Italy. In turn that lower profile may simply reflect the fact that child abuse is less common in those countries. However, it may instead be a function of a greater cultural unwillingness to recognise the extent of oppression within those societies associated with massive levels of child abuse; sources of social oppression deriving from poverty, age and gender.

In the light of this discussion, it is particularly interesting to turn to the last country in our survey: Denmark. For here we can see a conjunction between many of the issues we have raised earlier in the chapter. On the one hand, at the end of the nineteenth century and beginning of the twentieth century Denmark developed very similar structures for recognising and dealing with child maltreatment as were found in both England and Wales and Ireland. Moreover, we have noted that those structures played an important role in maintaining the profile of child maltreatment as a social issue in the latter two countries despite considerable resistances, especially in Ireland. Harder's account of the situation in Denmark suggests that child maltreatment has similarly remained an issue of considerable social significance across time in Denmark, even if the reasons for that significance have not remained constant.

Meanwhile, during the twentieth century the Danish welfare system has in many respects developed characteristics associated with "Social Democratic" welfare regimes, including relatively generous service provision, largely state-funded and explicitly designed to promote social cohesion. In this context, it is not surprising that Danish measures to address child abuse have to a large extent become subsumed within the more general aim of providing positive and supportive social work services for all children which we have also noted in relation to Finland - and which we have contrasted with England and Wales and to some extent with Ireland.

Yet, as Harder points out, this very positive third stage of social reform in Denmark may have been conceived in a period of economic prosperity, but it was realized in a period of economic depression which has to some extent continued to the present day as is the case in many other European countries. By contrast, Finnish welfare expansion seems to have initially lagged behind some of its Nordic neighbours and then grown more rapidly than many of them in the 1980s (Kangas 1994). It appears that the current serious financial difficulties of Finland only began to impinge on the welfare situation at the very end of the eighties and in the early nineties, no doubt partly exacerbated by the economic collapse of the Soviet Empire. Harder's account suggests that financial pressure on welfare provision has been a factor for considerably longer in Denmark. These differences between the economic profiles of Denmark and Finland, together with the apparently more deeply rooted awareness of child maltreatment as a serious social problem in Denmark, may go some way towards explaining certain divergences portrayed in the accounts of these two allegedly "Social Democratic" welfare regimes provided by Harder and Tuomisto and Vuori-Karvia. We will mention three here.

First, it is clear from the material presented in this volume that there has been considerably more professional attention paid to child abuse in Denmark than in Finland as reflected both in research and practice. In other words, although in both countries there is a tendency to a lack of differentiation between services for child abuse and for child care generally, this tendency seems to be stronger in Finland than in Denmark.

Secondly, and more specifically, the same seems to be true in relation to sexual abuse. After all, a "backlash" to sexual abuse seems to have occurred in Denmark, similar to that which has taken place in England and Wales. It may also be significant that both Harder and Pringle in relation to their own countries address the issue as to whether a concern with sexual abuse has to some extent "drowned out" from public and professional discourse other forms of abuse. None of these issues arises in the Finnish account.

Thirdly, Harder's account indicates that a targeting of service provision is currently a more salient feature of the picture in Denmark than so far has been the case in Finland. Such targeting, of course, is also one of the hallmarks of British welfare systems and is characteristic of "Neo-liberal" regimes.

In making these points we are not seeking to portray Denmark's welfare profile in a simplistic fashion as being closer to England than to Finland or as closer to a "neo-liberal" welfare regime than a "social democratic" one. Looked at in relative terms from the material in this volume, one has to acknowledge that in relation to the protection of children generally, Denmark still probably has far more in common with Finland than with either England and Wales, Ireland or Italy. We are, however, trying to show here, as we have throughout this chapter, that comparative issues regarding the protection of children must be seen as complex and multi-dimensional.

The picture in this section of the chapter is indeed complex. We have seen that there are overlaps in the dynamics of welfare provision between virtually all the countries surveyed in the book. Even the two most disparate countries in almost all respects, Italy/England and Wales, bear some similarity in the sense that for very different reasons there are massive doubts about how far each of them offers much positive assistance to abused children.

Ireland shares some close cultural features with both Italy and with England and Wales: for historical and structural reasons its protective services seem nearer to the latter than the former, whilst retaining its own characteristics and so far avoiding the worst excesses of English Child Protection.

In terms of recognising child abuse as a major social issue both Ireland and Denmark have something in common with England. Despite strong forces seeking to repress the extent of child abuse in Ireland, recognition is now considerable compared to many other European countries for a variety of historical and cultural reasons. Finland has perhaps less in common with these three in terms of recognition but by far the lowest level awareness seems to exist in Italy.

As regards the pattern of provision, England and Wales are poles apart from Finland. In the former, general child care provision has become almost exclusively focused on child abuse investigation with few resources directed to preventative or therapeutic services for maltreated children; and almost no attention has been paid to the positive promotion of children's well-being. Finland has taken a much broader and positive approach to child care provision, services for maltreated children largely being subsumed within those for the support of families generally.

The down-side of this picture as far as Finland is concerned may have two aspects: how long can the Finnish approach be afforded? Does the Finnish approach deny the realities of child abuse in their society?

Perhaps the real tragedy of the situation in England and Wales is that the enormity of the problem has been more fully realised there than anywhere else in Western Europe but the system designed to deal with it is wholly inadequate.

As we have noted, there may be considerable denial of child abuse in Italy for structural/ideological reasons and this is probably reflected in the variable but generally low level of service provision. The latter however can also be attributed to several other historical and cultural factors.

Whilst recognition of the problem is clearly greater in Ireland than in either Italy or Finland, service provision in Ireland is limited by resources and by the ongoing cultural resistance to the issue. A struggle seems to be occurring to develop a distinctive Irish response to the problem: one which acknowledges its size but which avoids the bureaucratic ineffectuality of the English response.

Finally we have seen how the situation in Denmark in many ways encapsulates the tensions which exist between all these themes: in some respects Denmark shares more in common with England and Wales and Ireland, whilst on other dimensions more with Finland. As with all these countries its responses to child maltreatment are an ongoing and changing outcome of its own complex cultural, social, political and economic trajectory.

Mention of trajectories, draws us to the final theme of this concluding chapter: in the light of all the above, what are the likely future trajectories of systems for protecting children in our five countries, and also perhaps, what ought those trajectories to be?

Future trajectories

Each of the chapter authors has made an attempt to provide pointers for the future. For instance, while Buckley is clear about some of the ongoing problems with protection of children in Ireland, she remains quite positive about the future. She suggests that the 1991 legislative framework, the newly-encouraged public and professional awareness of child abuse, the developments in professional training and the burgeoning amount of good quality research on the topic should ensure that children in Ireland will be protected more thoroughly than at any previous time.

No doubt that is a very sound appraisal. Nevertheless, in the context of the English experience one also wonders how far economic, media and other pressures may force Ireland further down the Child Protection route with all the negative consequences associated with it.

Bini and Toselli are not apparently optimistic about prospects for Italy. In particular they identify two major ongoing problems regarding the future. One is an issue we have already mentioned in relation to Ireland: financial constraints.

Given that service provision in this field is already at a very low level in Italy and given the severe financial problems of the Italian economy, apart from additional EMU pressure on the national budget, then this problem is acute. The other difficulty identified by the two Italian contributors is the inadequacy of Italian structures for dealing with the growing number of children from marginalized groups who require protection. As we have noted above, such difficulties are not confined to Italy. However, as Bini and Toselli make clear, the situation in Italy is again particularly acute because Italy to a considerable extent still relies on informal social networks for the provision of welfare: and extended, effective social networks are precisely what many marginalized groups in Italy lack.

We might also wonder how the problem of child abuse can be more meaningfully placed on Italian public and professional agendas in the context of the profound ideological and cultural resistances mentioned by Bini and Toselli. Such agenda-setting is now occurring in Ireland, a country which shares with Italy many of those sources of resistance. However, we have already pointed out that other structural, cultural and historical factors specific to Ireland mediate the resistance there - and indeed that resistance is still considerable in Ireland as Buckley notes.

Turning to the future in Finland, we find that Tuomisto and Vuori-Karvia identify at least one problem which is by now rather familiar to us: money. For there seems to be an imminent danger of major cuts in the funding which has maintained Finland's relatively generous, positive and supportive child welfare policies. The other potential issue identified by the two Finnish contributors as likely to impact upon the Finnish situation is interesting in view of our earlier discussion: they suggest a much greater public and professional awareness of the size and importance of child abuse may develop there. They seem to imply that the combination of these two factors may lead to a pattern of service provision for child abuse which is far more differentiated from general child welfare policies than is the case at present in Finland.

In the light of what we have seen in other countries, such a development might be a mixed blessing. On the one hand, we have argued that the relatively low level of awareness about child abuse in Finland is problematic and that purely supportive measures for families may not always be effective in countering child abuse, particularly sexual abuse. So changes in these areas are to be welcomed. On the other hand, we have seen that in England and Wales awareness of the issue is high and that service provision is extremely differentiated. And yet the system in England and Wales appears to be highly inefficient in terms of protecting the mass of children who are abused. So, if Finland for a variety of reasons does move towards more of an English approach, then the outlook there may not be at all positive.

Turning to England and Wales, Pringle's survey suggests that while the existing Child Protection model is thoroughly discredited, the more welfare-oriented family support model now advocated by the government seems equally doomed to failure. That prognosis is based on three arguments. First, he notes that such family support models have already operated in many continental countries such as Belgium, France, Germany and Austria: in all of them there is evidence that this kind of approach provides inadequate protection to children particularly in cases of sexual abuse. We might wonder in passing whether there are any implications here for other countries which operate models of protection based largely on the idea of family support such as Finland, Sweden and (to a lesser extent) Denmark.

Pringle's second argument is that the British government's advocacy of a family support approach may well be fuelled primarily by a desire to cut expenditure, whereas a truly supportive child care policy is bound to be expensive.

Thirdly and finally, Pringle suggests that the real levels of child abuse in society are so massive that no provision centred on professional services could possibly cope, even with huge funding. For this and other reasons he advocates a radical policy which places service users and adequately-funded and supported community resources at the centre of provision.

Interestingly, this enabling approach has much in common with Harder's "third way" as a view of the future in Denmark. However, Harder is usefully realistic in assessing the major problems with instituting such an approach. She notes the intransigence of problems in a minority of families which might overwhelm this model (as they overwhelm every other model), as well as the massive changes which this enabling model would require in the approach/ethics of social workers - and in their education.

We would not argue that there is only one way forward for the protection of children which should apply to all countries. For such an argument would run counter to our central belief that each country and its welfare system is a unique, and ever-changing, outcome of a specific set of historical, cultural, social, political and economic experiences. On the other hand, it is clear from the material in this book that child abuse poses many common problems and that the ways of tackling it are beset with difficulties which are also often surprisingly similar.

As we stand here in the closing years of a century which has seen far too much transnational conflict, we believe the scope for transnational sharing in the eradication of this particularly enormous and pernicious social problem, child abuse, is massive. That belief lies at the heart of this book and of the european network from which it has been born.

References

Ahmad, B. "Black perspectives in social work", Venture Press, 1990.

Armstrong, H. and Hollows. A. "Responses to child abuse in the EC" in Hill, M. (ed.) "Social work and the European Community", Jessica Kingsley Publishers, 1991.

Barn, R. "Black children in the public care system", Batsford, 1993.

Cannan, C. "Changing families, changing welfare", Harvester Wheatsheaf, 1992.

Cochrane, A. and Clarke, J. (eds.) "Comparing welfare states: Britain in international context", Sage, 1993.

Cooper, A., Hetherington, R., Baistow, K., Pitts, J., and Spriggs, A. "Positive child protection: a view from abroad", Russell House Publishing, 1995.

Esping-Andersen, G. "The three worlds of welfare capitalism", Polity Press, 1990.

Esping-Andersen, G. (ed.) "Welfare states in transition: national adaptions in global economies", Sage,1996.

Ferrera, M. "The 'southern model' of welfare in Europe", Journal of European Social Policy, vol.6(1), 1996.

Finkelhor, D. "The scope of the problem" in Murray, K. and Gough, D.A. (eds.) "Intervening in child sexual abuse", Scottish Academic Press, 1991.

Ginsburg, N. "Divisions of welfare: a critical introduction to comparative social policy", Sage, 1992.

Hallett, C. "Child abuse; an academic overview" in
Kingston, P. and Penhale, B. (eds.) "Family violence and the caring professions", Macmillan, 1995.

Jeffreys, S. "Anticlimax: a feminist perspective on the sexual revolution", The Women's Press, 1990.

Kangas, O. "The merging of welfare state models", Journal of European Social Policy, vol.4(2), 1994.

Kelly, L. "Surviving sexual violence", Polity Press, 1988.

Leibfried, S. "Towards a European welfare state? on integrating poverty regimes into the European Community" in Jones, C. (ed.) "new perpectives on the welfare state in Europe", Routledge, 1993.

Lorenz, W. "Social work in a changing Europe", Routledge, 1994.

Mitchell, M. and Russell, D. "Race, citizenship and "Fortress Europe" in Brown, P. and Crompton, R. (eds.) "Economic restructuring and social exclusion", UCL Press, 1994.

Munday, B. and Ely, P. (eds.) "Social care in Europe", Prentice Hall: Harvester Wheatsheaf, 1996.

Parton, C. and Parton, N. "Child protection, the law and dangerousness" in Stevenson, O. (ed.) "Child abuse: public policy and professional practice", Harvester Wheatsheaf, 1989.

Parton, N. "Child protection, family support and social work", Child and Family Social Work, vol.1(1), 1996.

Pringle, K. "Child sexual abuse committed by welfare personnel: British and European perspectives", paper presented at fourth European conference on child abuse and neglect, University of Padova, 1993.

Pringle, K. "Men, masculinities and social welfare". UCL Press, 1995.

Pringle, K. "Protecting children against sexual abuse: a third way?", paper presented at conference on "Human services in crisis: national and international issues", Fitzwilliam College, University of Cambridge, September 1996.

Pringle, K. "Children and social welfare in Europe", Open University Press, (forthcoming) 1997.

Rex J, "Race and ethnicity in Europe" in Bailey, J. (ed.) "Social europe", Longman, 1992.

Ruxton, S. "Children in Europe", NCH Action For Children, 1996.

Segal, L. "Slow motion: changing masculinities, changing men", Virago Press, 1990.

Spano, A. "The economic and cultural dimensions of poverty in Italy: the implications for social policy", social Work in Europe, vol.3(2), 1996.

Spicker, P. "Solidarity" in Room, G. (ed.) "Towards A European Welfare State", SAUS, 1991.
Stevenson, O. (ed.) "Child abuse: public policy and professional practice", Harvester Wheatsheaf, 1989.

About The Authors

Laura Bini teaches methods and techniques of social work in the courses of Social Work at the university of Florence. She has worked with clients having mental health and addiction problems. Experienced in family mediation she is now training and supervising social workers of the public services.

Helen Buckley is a lecturer in the Department of Applied Social Studies in Trinity College Dublin. She is completing a Ph.D. on child protection practice, and teaches in this area and also in mental health. She has worked as a social worker in the fields of child care, mental health and disability. Recent publications include 'Child abuse guidelines in Ireland: for whose protection?' in *Protecting Irish Children: investigation, protection and welfare* (1996) edited by Harry Ferguson and Tony McNamara. During 1996 she co-authored a piece of commissioned research, soon to be published, which evaluates child protection practice in an Irish Health Board region.

Margit Harder is Reader in social work and psychiatry at Aalborg University. She has practised as a social worker for ten years in child psychiatry. Her main research area is: child care, child protection and underprivileged families. She is participating in networks between professionals in the child/family field at a national, an inter-nordic and an inter-european level.

Keith Pringle is currently Reader in Social Policy at the University of Sunderland in the north east of England. For ten years he practised as a qualified social worker in the field of child and adolescent care. His research interests are: child care, gender studies, anti-oppressive practice service user enablement and comparative social policy. He played a central role in developing the Erasmus/Socrates network which is the basis of this study.

Monica Toselli is researcher in psychology at the university of Florence and teaches developmental psychology. Her research interests pertain to infants and parenting.

Riitta Tuomisto has a Master's degree in Political Science. She is a social worker and a lecturer of social sciences and specialises in teaching social work and child protection at Vantaa Polytechnic. The Department of Social Studies has many projects with social work practice agencies of which she has been involved in two. Her main interest in recent years is a partnership with social work field offices and social workers in the area of child protection.

Elina Vuori-Karvia has been working as a senior lecturer in Vantaa Institute of Social Studies since 1988. Her responsibilities have also included positions as Assistant Principal and Department Head at the same institute. Her main teaching subjects are in the areas of psychology and child care. She graduated from Helsinki University with Master's degrees both in Psychology and Education. She has also received the Professional Teacher Certification. During the academic year 1990-1991 she furthered her studies at the Department of Psychology of Vanderbilt University in the United States. Now she is finishing a further degree in psychology at Helsinki University.